Urbit Systems Technical Journal

First paperback edition January 2026.
ISSN 2997-9137

urbitsystems.tech
groundwire.io
urbit.org

Published by West Martian Limited Company
Cheyenne, Wyoming

westmartian.com

Vol. 3, No. 1, 2026 : The Journal of Solid-State Computing

Urbit Systems Technical Journal

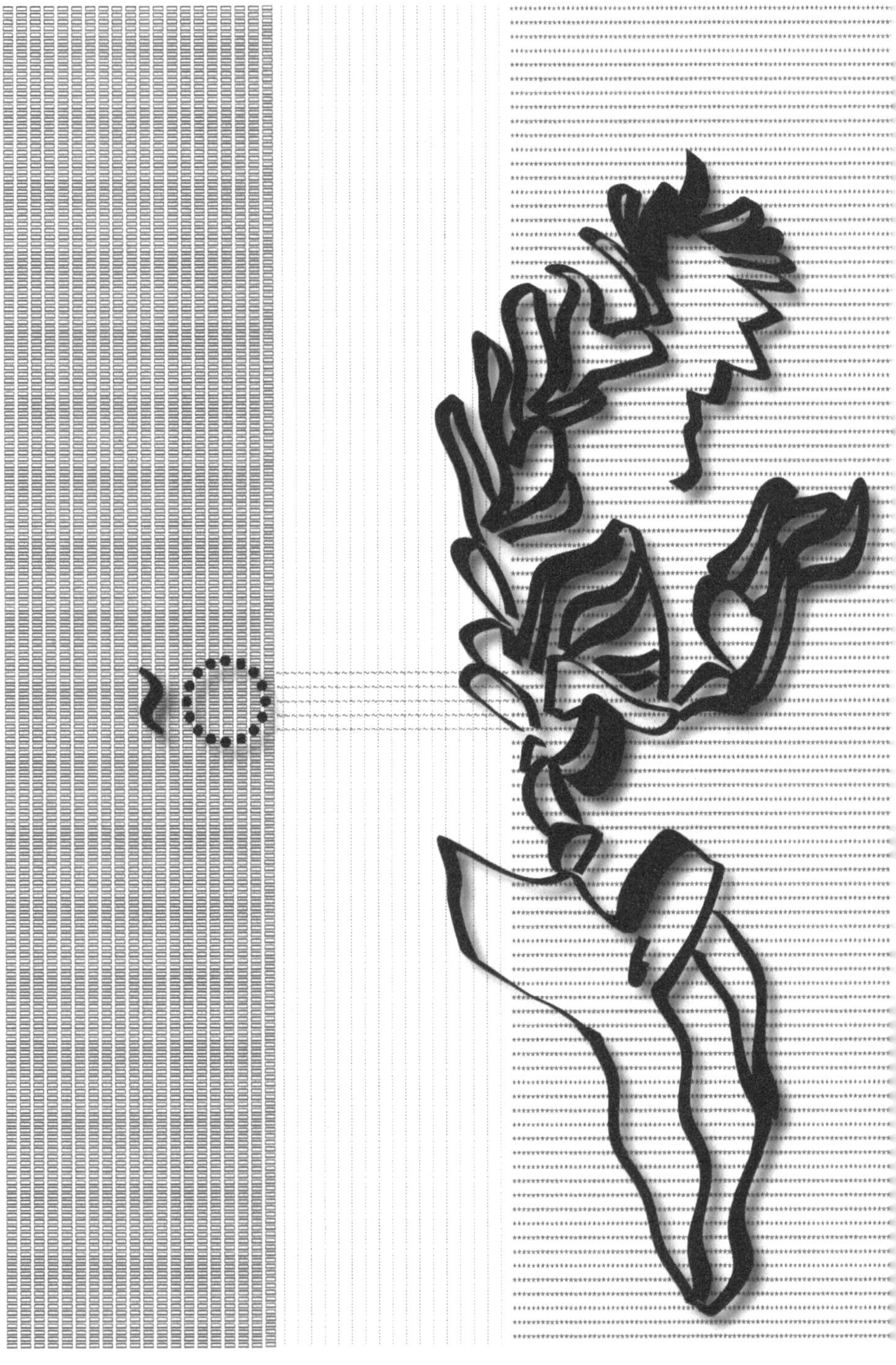

My first encounter with Urbit was like Mr. Electrico knighting twelve-year-old Ray Bradbury with a charged sword and charging him to "live forever!" The vision of unfolding but comprehensible complexity was a (friendly) siren's song that has led to rewarding professional relationships and deep friendships. Shape rotator programming has become a lifelong passion and fertile ground of exploration.

This issue of the *Urbit Systems Technical Journal* unveils technical descriptions of significant milestones in Urbit's ongoing development. ~rovnys-ricfer, ~master-morzod, ~watter-parter, ~dinleb-rambep, ~norsyr-torryn, and ~hastuc-dibtux detail the design and implementation of Urbit's named data networking scheme, Directed Messaging, a core component of the 2023 "Neo-Urbit" vision. ~dozreg-toplud expounds the long-anticipated "subject knowledge analysis" paradigm for Hoon static analysis, proposed several years ago by ~ritpub-sipsyl and long a target for more efficient Hoon compilation to the Nock combinator calculus. ~hanfel-dovned presents portions of the Groundwire proposal for a revision of Urbit's peer-to-peer schema beyond Azimuth, a topic of ongoing technical interest in the Urbit developer community. ~ticlys-monlun and ~lagrev-nocfep explain how the Nock serialization mechanism for nouns works in detail. And ~nomryg-nilref reveals in great detail his monumental labor of love that is Obelisk, a return to E. F. Codd's relational algebra and SQL. Each article represents years of design and engineering work, and we are proud to present them to the Urbit community.

As of 2025, *USTJ* has become a sponsored project of the Groundwire Foundation, a new nonprofit entity dedicated to Urbit's core development and improving support for Bitcoin integrations into the Urbit ecosystem. We are grateful for their patronage and the educational and documentary mandate.

Computer science happens in the trenches.

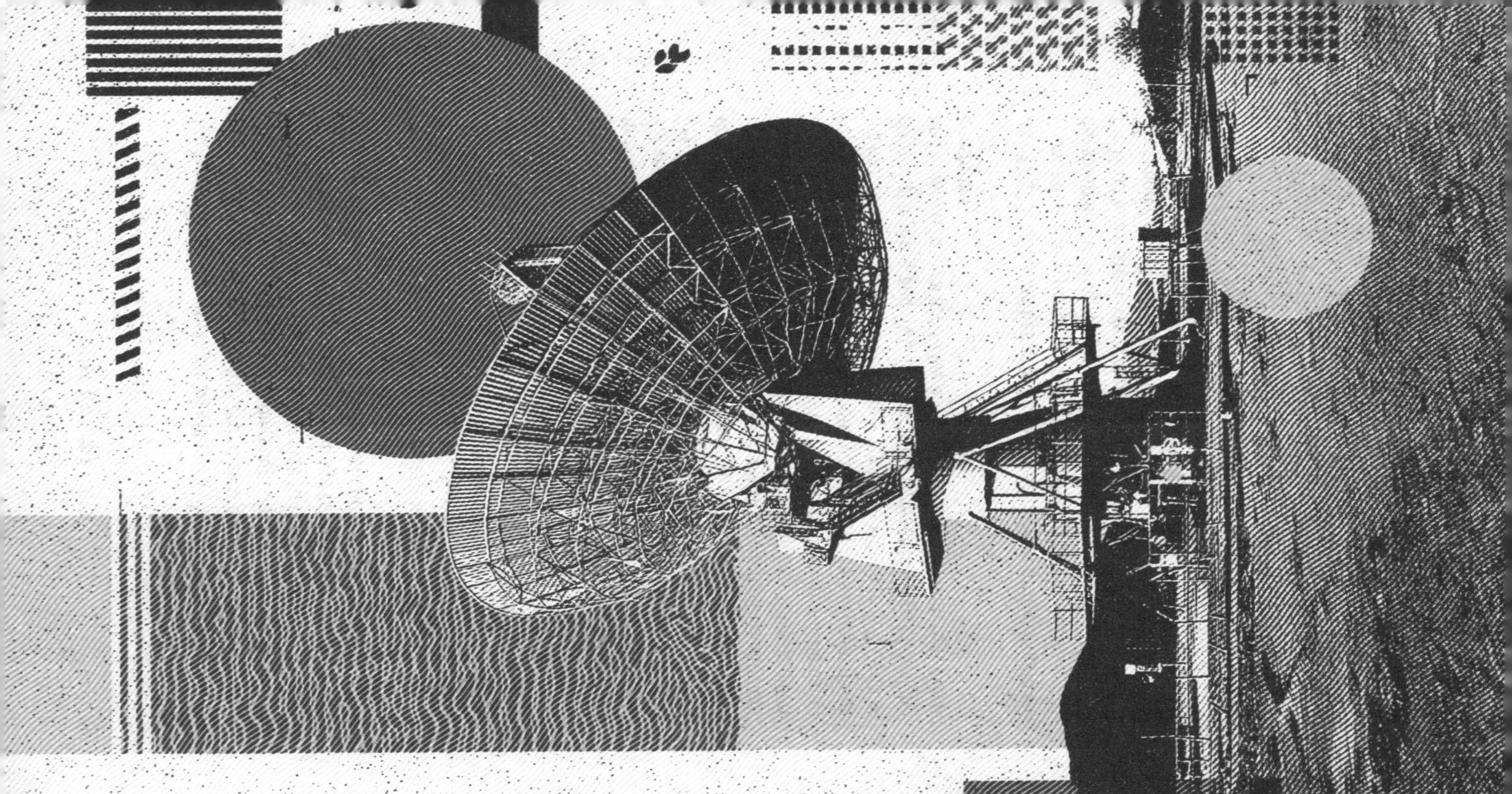

DIR MES

Urbit's networking protocol was redesigned achieving over 100x throughput improvements while implementing content-centric networking in a production peer-to-peer system. Unlike address-based routing, all network operations (queries and commands) are expressed as remote namespace reads. Urbit's immutable scry namespace enables efficient caching, deterministic encryption, and stateless publishing, while a pre-distributed PKI eliminates handshake overhead for single-roundtrip transactions.

Directed Messaging

Ted Blackman ~rovnys-ricfer,*
Joe Bryan ~master-morzod,†
Luke Champine ~watter-parter,*
Pyry Kovanen ~dinleb-rambep,†
Jose Cisneros ~norsyr-torryn,†
Liam Fitzgerald ~hastuc-dibtux‡
* Martian Engineering,
† Tlon Corporation,
‡ Axiomatic Systems

Abstract

Urbit's networking protocol was redesigned achieving over 100× throughput improvements while implementing content-centric networking in a production peer-to-peer system. Unlike address-based routing, all network operations (queries and commands) are expressed as remote namespace reads. Urbit's immutable scry namespace enables efficient caching, deterministic encryption, and stateless publishing, while a pre-distributed PKI eliminates handshake overhead for single-roundtrip transactions. Lockstep Streaming, a novel scale-invariant packet authentication scheme using binary numeral trees, maintains authentication integrity across variable MTU sizes at relay hops. The Lackman traversal pattern enables constant-space streaming authentication. Directed routing simplifies peer discovery and NAT traversal compared to previous approaches, while source-independent routing minimizes relay state. Begun in 2023 under the auspices of the Urbit Foundation and deployed in early 2025, Directed Messaging represents the first large-scale deployment of content-centric networking.

Urbit Systems Technical Journal III:1 (2026): 1–41.
Address author correspondence to ~rovnys-ricfer.

Contents

1 Introduction

The Directed Messaging project was a fundamental overhaul of Urbit's networking stack. It rewrote the protocol definition and the protocol implementation, split between Hoon code inside Arvo (the Urbit overlay OS), and C code in Vere (the Urbit runtime).[1] Directed Messaging addressed several major limitations of Urbit's previous networking stack: it increased throughput by over 100×, improved peer discovery reliability, enabled the scalability of content delivery, and introduced a modular internal architecture that reduced implementation complexity. Directed Messaging is an encrypted, authenticated, peer-to-peer, packet-switched, message-oriented, connectionless, content-centric, transactional network protocol with its own congestion control, transmission control, and packet-level authentication. It was deployed to the Urbit network in early 2025.

These improvements were driven by Directed Messaging's total adherence to a request-response discipline throughout the stack, bundled with heavy use of Urbit's immutable referentially-transparent global namespace, called the "scry namespace". Every network message is either a request for data at a "scry path" (Urbit's equivalent of a URL), or an authenticated response that includes the data at that path. This is true at the message layer and the packet layer, and for both reads (queries) and writes (commands).

Before Directed Messaging, the bandwidth Urbit was able to utilize was extremely limited, maxing out in the hundreds of kilobytes per second. It lacked orders of magnitude of perfor-

[1]The original Ames protocol is described in early detail in the Urbit whitepaper (`~sorreg-namtyv` et al., 2016) with further elaboration in `~rovnys-ricfer`, "Eight Years After the Whitepaper", USTJ vol. 1 iss. 1, pp. 1–46.

mance in order to make effective use of commodity networking hardware, such as on a laptop or cloud instance. With Directed Messaging, Urbit's networking speed was able to reach over 1 Gibit/s on commodity hardware, sufficient for the vast majority of contemporary personal use cases.

Directed Messaging managed to improve throughput while preserving Urbit's already-good latency performance. For small messages, a network transaction is accomplished in one roundtrip: a command sent one way, followed by an acknowledgment the other way. Due to Urbit's public key infrastructure (PKI) being disseminated to all nodes *a priori* from a Byzantine fault-tolerant source (the Ethereum blockchain and a bespoke L2 for economic efficiency), no cryptographic handshake is needed for two Urbit nodes (called "ships" in Urbit lingo) to begin communication – even their first exchange is a single roundtrip.

In addition to performance improvements, Directed Messaging scales better by leveraging runtime caching to disseminate data to many clients simultaneously. This strategy is particularly effective within Urbit's immutable scry namespace. Directed Messaging also introduces a new procedure for peer discovery and routing that is much more reliable and performant than the previous setups. It deals better with NAT traversal and with using supernodes as relays more efficiently and reliably.

All of this is done by simplifying the basic networking structure to enforce a rigid request-response discipline throughout the entire system. In addition to that, it also places all network messages, including acknowledgments and commands, in addition to responses for queries asking for data, into the referentially transparent scry namespace. This makes Urbit's entire networking stack a named data networking system, which is also called content-centric networking. As far as the authors know, Directed Messaging is the very first production deployment of a content-centric networking protocol, as well as the deployment with the largest number of nodes. Not only that, its content-centricity preserves the immutability of Urbit's namespace throughout the stack. The immutability is key to the scalability improvements and reliability improvements, and it also helps with single-threaded performance.

Along the way, we designed and implemented a novel scheme for streaming packet authentication. This helps prevent denial-of-service attacks that could forge individual packets and spoof them in order to invalidate a large download. This attack is prevented by authenticating every packet, but unlike the previous version of Urbit's networking stack, which authenticated each packet with a signature (meaning one signature for every kilobyte of data, which was extremely inefficient), there's only one signature per message. A Merkelization scheme using binary numeral trees is used to authenticate the packets within that message (`~watter-parter`, 2021).

This achieves a property that, to our knowledge, has not been demonstrated in prior packet authentication schemes: the ability to handle a different maximum transmission unit (MTU) at each hop in a relay chain without losing packet-level authentication. It is a scale-invariant packet-authentication scheme, and it also has good memory use characteristics, due to a novel algorithm based on the "Lackman" scale-invariant tree-traversal pattern developed by the authors. A relay receiving packets of one size and emitting packets of another size only needs to hold one large packet in memory while streaming (e. g. if receiving 1 kiB packets and sending 16kiB packets, it only needs to store 16 kiB of packet data at a time). It can seamlessly handle any MTU that is one kilobyte, two kilobytes, or any power-of-two number of kilobytes above that, up to 128 MiB.

Another advantage of the Directed Messaging protocol is that much more of the logic can be offloaded from the Urbit operating system, Arvo, into the runtime. This enables decoupling between the formal specification, which is written in Nock, and implementation, which is written in C. This is in keeping with the spirit of Urbit's "jet" system that separates mechanism and policy for code execution. The most straightforward advantage of this decoupling is that each packet can be processed ephemerally, without incurring a disk write as in previous versions of Urbit's network protocol – that was a severe bottleneck on the maximum throughput. The implementation in the runtime could be swapped out with another implementation written in another language, the congestion control algorithm could be swapped out, and parallelism strategies could readily be employed to increase multicore CPU utilization. The implementation that was deployed contains a major optimization: specialized arena allocators to reduce memory management overhead.

2 High-Level Protocol Design

2.1 Request/Response, Namespace Reads

The protocol design is based off the idea of a remote namespace read, wherein a "subscriber" ship requests data from a "publisher" ship, and the publisher sends that data as the response. The publisher ship makes the data available over the network by assigning it a path in Urbit's scry namespace and setting permissions appropriately (permissioning will be described fully in a later section). The subscriber ship, then, can download data from another ship by sending it a request for the data at a path and waiting for the response.

A network roundtrip is conceived of as a request, followed by a response. The request consists of a "scry request", i. e. a request for data at a scry path. An example scry path is `/~zod/1/2/c/x/~2025.9.22/sys/kelvin`. A scry path immutably names a datum, in this case the `sys.kelvin` file published by `~zod` (at `rift=1` and `life=2`), within the `%c` kernel module (Clay, the revision control system), with request type `%x` (request file contents), and with timestamp at the start of the day on September 22, 2025. When a ship receives a scry request over the network, it can respond by sending a "scry response" containing the datum bound to that path.

Over the network, a network request is a single UDP packet that encodes a scry path, limited to 384 characters so the request packet always fits into the internet-standard 1500-byte MTU (maximum transmission unit). A scry response may consist of a single packet, or multiple packets, depending on the size of the datum bound to that path. If the datum is 1kiB or less, the response is encoded into a single UDP packet. Otherwise, the first scry response packet contains only the first 1kiB of the datum, along with a fixed-width field containing the number of bits in the whole datum.

If the subscriber ship receives a response indicating the datum is multi-packet, it switches modes and begins requesting the remainder of the datum, one kiB at a time. Each request for a kiB of data is itself a fully-fledged namespace read request, where the path in the request contains the path of the whole datum as well as the chunk size being requested (configured to 1 kiB over the public internet, but this could be increased to any power of 2 kiB's up to 128 MiB, for other environments, such as intra-datacenter). The protocol definition does not require those fragment requests to be sent in any particular order or according to any particular congestion control algorithm. The current implementation uses a packet-switched variant of the TCP NewReno congestion control algorithm, written in C in Urbit's runtime, to manage multi-packet reads. The message-level authentication is sent in the first response packet. Each subsequent packet is authenticated as being part of that message by using the LockStep streaming authentication scheme, described in a later section.

This remote read flow is a "pure read": handling a read request does not require the publisher ship to change any persistent state. But a general-purpose network protocol needs to be able to express commands, not just reads. Directed Messaging builds commands out of reads. A command is conceived of as two reads, one in each direction:

1. The ship sending the command makes the command datum available within its own scry namespace, so the receiving ship has the ability to read the command by sending a remote read request.

2. The ship that receives the command, after attempting to execute the command, makes the command's result available within its namespace, so the sending ship has the ability to read the result (hereafter called the "ack") by sending a remote read request. A result can be success ("ack") or an error datum ("naxplanation", named after "nack" for negative acknowledgment).

This approach is conceptually clean but immediately presents two practical challenges. The first is triggering: how does the receiving ship *know* to request the command datum from the sending ship? There are many ships on the network; it would be absurdly impractical to send requests to all of them on the off-chance that one or two of them have an outstanding command for us. The second challenge is latency: a naive implementation would imply every command requires two network roundtrips, one to remote-read the command and one to remote-read the command's result (ack or naxplanation). If so, that would be unfortunate, since Urbit's previous networking required only one roundtrip for a command and ack, in the common case of a small (≤1 kiB) command datum, and unneeded roundtrips are anathema to a good user experience (Cheshire, 1996).

Fortunately, we can solve both problems with one weird trick. We add a "request type" bit to each network request packet indicating whether it is a read or a command, and if it is a command, it includes not only the scry request path, but also a scry response containing the first 1 kiB of the command datum. When the receiving ship's runtime receives the packet, it looks at the 'request-type' bit to determine how to handle the packet.

If the incoming request packet is a read, the runtime performs a read request on the Arvo OS by firing its `+peek` arm, a Nock function that reads from Arvo's namespace. This read request does not trigger any disk writes and could be run in parallel with other reads and with an Arvo event. The runtime then encodes the result of this read as a scry response packet and sends it back to the IP and port that sent the request.

If the packet is a command, the runtime injects the packet as a stateful Arvo "event" by firing its `+poke` arm (a Nock function that sends an event or command for Arvo to process, producing effects and a new Arvo OS with a modified state). When this event completes, one of the effects it produces can be a scry response packet containing the ack, which the runtime will send back to the IP and port that sent the request.

If the command datum fits within 1 kiB, the entire command is sent in the first packet, recapturing the single-roundtrip flow for a command and an ack. Multi-packet commands are downloaded by the commanded ship using the same congestion control as downloading any other potentially large datum – and, importantly, those incremental downloads do not necessarily trigger unnecessarily frequent disk writes.

3 Routing

3.1 Directed Routing

The Directed Messaging protocol gets its name from its routing scheme, which treats each bidirectional communication between two Urbit ships as directed, like a directed edge in a graph. For each request/response roundtrip, one ship is the requester, and the other is the responder, and that distinction is known at every layer of the system. Making this directionality known to routing enables a routing paradigm where a response packet traces the exact same relay path through the network as the request path, in the reverse order. Previous Urbit networking protocols used the opposite paradigm: "criss-cross routing", so-called because both request and response could be routed through the destination ship's "sponsor", i. e. the supernode ship ("galaxy" root node or "star" infrastructure node) responsible for relaying packets to that ship. In contrast, in directed routing, the request and the response both use the same relay: the responder ship's sponsor. See Figure 1 for a comparison of the two routing strategies.

3.2 Relaying

Making the directedness of communication legible to relays and Urbit runtimes allows the protocol to be a faithful, if Urbit-specific, Named Data Networking (NDN) protocol, which had been Urbit's stated goal since 2010. A Directed Messaging request packet acts as an NDN "interest" packet, and a response packet acts as an NDN "data" packet.

The NDN family of protocols, created by Van Jacobson et al. in the mid-2000s, differs from traditional networking protocols

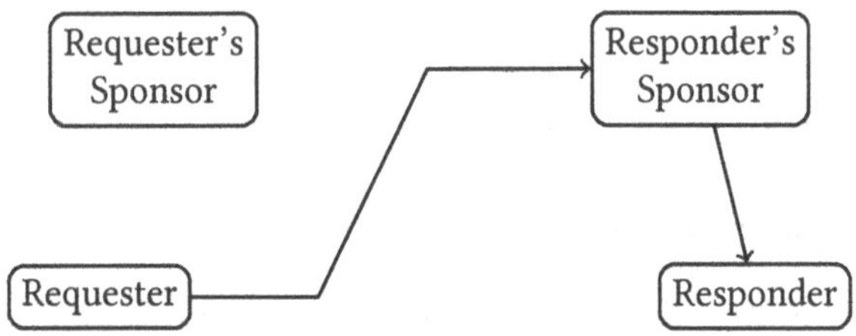

(a) Request (same for both directed and criss-cross routing).

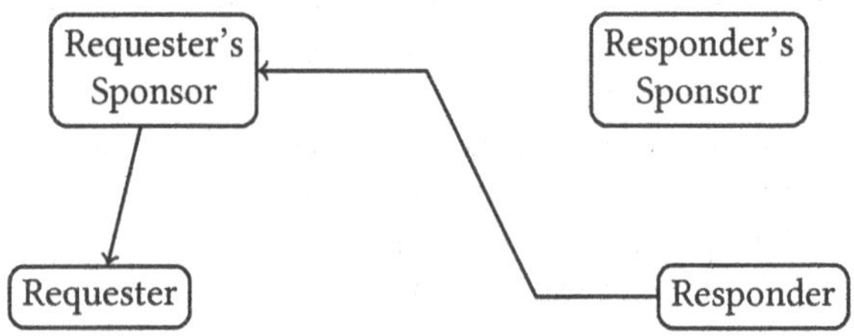

(b) Response (criss-cross routing).

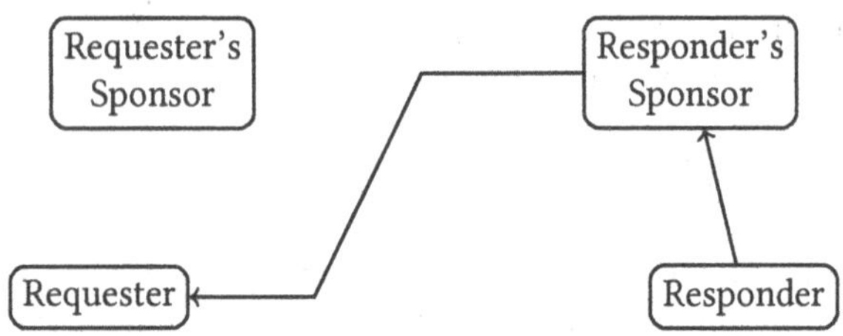

(c) Response (directed routing).

Figure 1: Routing strategies.

in that an interest packet has no sender address field – the identity of the sender of a request is unknown to the network. Instead, a receiver (relay or server) remembers "where" it heard the request from, and sends the response back to that. The notion of "where" varies depending on the layer of the stack the system is operating at: for an IP replacement, a relay would remember the physical interface (e. g. Ethernet port) on which it heard the incoming request. When building on top of IP and UDP, as Directed Messaging does, a receiver remembers the IP and port of the sender.

Previous Urbit network protocols still included the sender's Urbit identity in the request packets, failing to achieve the "source independence" property that defines NDN. Directed Messaging is completely source-independent for reads, and for commands, it piggybacks a source-independent response onto a source-independent request in such a way that the receiver does know which Urbit address sent the request, but not in a way that requires packet routing to know or use the source Urbit address.

Source independence lets the routing operate fully locally, without reference to or knowledge of anything beyond a single hop away in either direction. This minimizes the data storage and synchronization requirements for nodes, which could become significant at scale.

Source independence entails stateful routing. Directed Messaging adopts NDN's Pending Interest Table, which stores a mapping from each outstanding request to the IP and port that sent that request. If the request times out (after roughly 30 seconds), or the request is satisfied by a response, the request is deleted from the table.

Since responses are authenticated down to the packet level, and immutable (meaning no cache invalidation is ever needed, only eviction), it should be straightforward for relays to cache responses, enabling efficient content distribution through the network. At present, each Urbit ship's runtime has a cache for its own responses, but supernodes (galaxies and stars) do not yet cache responses from their sponsored ships.

3.3 Peer Discovery

Urbit is a peer-to-peer network. Only root nodes (galaxies) list their own IP addresses publicly (on the Ethereum blockchain); all other ships must be discovered on demand. When one ship first sends a request to another ship, it generally doesn't know at what IP and port that ship could be reached, and it also doesn't know if the ship is reachable directly, or behind a firewall and only reachable through its sponsor.

The criss-cross routing used in previous Urbit protocols was hard to work with in practice and suffered from inefficiencies and bugs. Directed Messaging has a simpler approach to peer discovery that is easier to reason about.

The main difficulties with criss-cross routing stem from the structure of the internet. Most residential internet connections live behind a firewall that blocks all unsolicited incoming UDP packets. A laptop at home can send an outgoing packet to some destination IP and port, and the router will relay response packets back to the laptop for some time afterward, usually 30 seconds, as long as those response packets come from that same destination IP and port.

A UDP-based peer-to-peer network, then, needs to include not only residential nodes but also nodes on the public internet, not behind firewalls. These nodes must be discoverable so that residential nodes can ping them every 25 seconds, to ensure the residential nodes can receive messages. In Urbit, these public nodes are the galaxies (root nodes) and stars (infrastructure nodes). For now, only galaxies perform routing, due to edge cases with two levels of supernodes in peer discovery using criss-cross routing – we expect Directed Messaging will unblock stars from participating in routing.

When communicating with another ship for the first time, a ship first sends the packet to the other ship's sponsoring galaxy, which has an open connection to its sponsored ship if it's online. The galaxy receives a ping every 25 seconds from its sponsored ship. Whenever the source IP and port change, the galaxy's runtime injects an Arvo event and its Arvo OS saves the sponsored ship's new location to disk.

In Directed Messaging, when the galaxy receives a packet

intended for one of its sponsored ships, it relays the packet. This uses the pending interest table described above to track the fact that there is an outstanding request that the galaxy is expecting to be honored by a response from the sponsored ship. The fundamental invariant of directed routing is that the response packet must trace the exact same path through the network as the request packet had, just reversed. Since this request had gone through this galaxy, the response must also route through the galaxy.

In Urbit's previous protocols, in contrast, the response would go directly from the sponsored ship back to the requesting ship, and also potentially through the requesting ship's sponsoring galaxy. This works in principle, but one drawback has to do with "route tightening" (described below): the response route only tightens to a direct route (without relays) if there are requests flowing in both directions; otherwise every response will flow through the requester's sponsor, even if the requester is not behind a firewall.

3.4 Route Tightening

It is better for performance, scaling, and individual sovereignty to obtain a direct route to another ship, rather than communicating through relays. In order to facilitate this, the system must automatically "tighten" a route over time to reduce the number of hops. Directed Messaging accomplishes this in the relay. When a relay receives a response packet (originally sent by a transivitely sponsored ship, but possibly through a relay once stars begin relaying packets), it appends the IP and port from which it heard that packet to the end of the packet before forwarding it to the requesting ship. Once the requesting ship receives this augmented packet, it knows the address appended to that packet is next hop in the relay chain. Once it knows that, when it sends packets to the responding ship, it can send them through the first hop in the relay chain (the receiving ship's galaxy), or to the next hop, which could be another relay or the ship itself.

In the current implementation, the requesting ship uses a simple procedure to decide which routes to send the packet on. It tracks the date of the last received packet from both the direct route and the route through the galaxy. A route is considered active if a packet has been received on it within the last five seconds. When the requesting ship goes to send a packet, if the direct route is active, it sends the packet on that route. Otherwise, it sends the packet through the galaxy and also sends a copy of the packet on the direct route as a probe.

This ensures continuity of communication when switching to or from a direct route, and it automatically tightens to the direct route if the direct route is responsive and loosens to the galaxy route if the direct route becomes unresponsive.

4 Authentication and Encryption

Directed Messaging is always authenticated and supports encryption in a number of different modes:

- **Unencrypted reads**: A ship can publish data into its namespace without encryption. Response messages are signed using the ship's private key. The signature attests to the scry binding: the pair of the scry path and the datum at that path.
- **One-to-One Encrypted Reads**: A ship can make data available to a single peer ship. Response messages are authenticated via an external hash-based message authentication code (HMAC) and internal signature. They are encrypted using a symmetric key derived from the Diffie-Hellman key exchange of the two ships' keys.
- **Commands**: Commands and their acks are both handled as one-to-one encrypted reads.
- **One-to-Many Encryption**: A ship can make data available to many ships by sharing an encryption key for that data to each ship using a one-to-one encrypted read. The requesting ship then uses that key to encrypt the request's scry path and decrypt the scry response.

The core encryption primitives consist of:

- `kdf`: BLAKE3, in its key derivation mode.
- `crypt`: XChaCha8, with its 24-byte nonce derived by processing the (arbitrary-length) input initialization vector (IV) using the key derivation function (`kdf`) with `"mesa-crypt-iv"` as the context string.

Messages and their paths are encrypted separately. First, `kdf` is used to derive an authentication key and encryption key from the shared secret. The authentication key is used to compute a 128-bit keyed BLAKE3 hash of the path; this serves as the Authenticated Encryption with Associated Data (AEAD) tag. The encryption key is then used to encrypt the path with `crypt`, using the tag as the IV. Concatenating the encrypted path and authentication tag yields a "sealed" path. The message itself is then encrypted with `crypt`, using the sealed path as the IV. Authentication of the message is achieved via a Merkle hashing scheme described later.

Directed Messaging's encryption scheme uses a variant of ChaCha20, XChaCha, with reduced rounds for performance. XChaCha is an extended-nonce variant of ChaCha that accepts a 192-bit nonce instead of the standard 96-bit nonce. However, rather than using the caller-provided initialization vector directly as the nonce, Directed Messaging first applies a BLAKE3 key derivation function to derive a deterministic 24-byte nonce from the IV using the context string `"mesa-crypt-iv"`. This XChaCha operation with 8 rounds then produces a derived key and extended nonce, which are subsequently used for the actual ChaCha encryption (also with 8 rounds) of the message payload. The use of 8 rounds instead of the standard 20 is a performance optimization – ChaCha's security margin allows for this reduction in cryptographic applications where the extreme paranoia of 20 rounds may be unnecessary (Aumasson, 2019), and the deterministic nonce derivation via BLAKE3 adds an additional layer of domain separation.

Because the scry namespace immutably binds paths to their message data, the path serves as a synthetic IV for the message, making encryption deterministic. This solves multiple problems. It (along with other principles of Directed Messaging) prevents replay attacks by construction. Every Directed Messaging packet is idempotent at the application level (a duplicate packet can trigger a duplicate ack and minor state changes in the runtime and Arvo kernel related to routing state, but it cannot modify anything visible to an application). It further removes the need for explicit nonce management, such as generating, storing, and transmitting an explicit nonce for each message. Not tracking nonces reduces the system's security attack surface area considerably, since nonce state mismanagement is a common source of vulnerabilities. Finally, supporting encrypted values in the namespace allows the system to implement encryption using overlay namespaces (described in more detail below), which provide a clean layering that separates encryption from other concerns.

Before transmission, a single `0x1` byte is appended to the encrypted message, called a "trailer byte". This solves a representation problem specific to Urbit's atom system. In Urbit, data is ultimately stored as "atoms": arbitrary-precision natural numbers. The atom system cannot distinguish between byte streams with equivalent numerical value; that is, it has no way to "say" `0x1000` instead of `0x1` or `0x1000000000` – all are numerically equivalent to 1.[2] Thus, if a ciphertext happens to end with one or more zero bytes, those would be stripped when the ciphertext is represented as an atom, corrupting the data. Appending a 0x1 byte ensures that the atom representation always preserves the full length of the ciphertext, including any trailing zeros. During decryption, the code verifies that the final byte is indeed `0x1` (which catches truncation or corruption) and then strips it before decrypting. This construction provides authenticated encryption properties through the deterministic relationship between the IV and nonce, ensuring that any tampering with the ciphertext or IV will result in decryption failure.

[2]Note the relative most-significant byte (MSB) order notation used here, contrary to Urbit's customary LSB order.

4.1 Message Authentication and Encryption Details

4.1.1 Overlay Namespaces

Each of the three privacy modes has its own "overlay namespace", i. e. a part of the scry namespace that somehow transforms values bound to a different part of the namespace. A path in an overlay namespace often consists of a path prefix containing the name of the overlay and any parameters needed for the transformation it performs on the datum at the overlaid path, followed by the overlaid path.

A handler function that deals with scry requests to the overlay namespace is free to parse transformation parameters out of the overlay prefix, inspect the overlaid path, make a scry request for the data at that path, make scry requests related to that path (such as existence checks for file paths), and run arbitrary code to transform the results. This is all possible because scry requests are purely functional by construction – they are deterministic functions of their inputs, with no hidden inputs, and there is no mechanism by which they could change Arvo state.

Directed Messaging uses overlay namespaces not only for privacy modes, but also to publish individual packets within a message. The packet's size (expressed as the log base 2 kiB, e. g. 3 for 8 kiB or 4 for 16 kiB) and fragment number (index within the message) are parameters to this overlay, which overlays the message's scry path.

Directed Messaging is the first Urbit kernel module to make heavy use of overlay namespaces in its design. They play an important role in maintaining boundaries between layers within the system: privacy is separated, by construction, from other concerns due to the isolation imposed by overlay namespaces. For example, an application can declare what privacy mode it wants to use for a piece of data it publishes, and the kernel enforces that by exposing it over the network using the appropriate overlay namespace.

4.1.2 `%publ` namespace (unencrypted public)

A value registered in the `%publ` namespace is intended to be publicly readable by anyone on the network. The message is not encrypted, but it is authenticated using signature authentication only (using a 64-byte Ed25519 signature calculated over the encoded beam path and the LSS root of the unencrypted jammed data). The publisher signs the message using their Ed25519 private key (extracted from their networking key), and the receiver verifies the signature using the publisher's Ed25519 public key retrieved from Azimuth. In this model, authenticity is provided by the signature, while confidentiality is not provided since the message is sent in plaintext.

The `%publ` namespace uses unencrypted paths with the structure:

```
/publ/[life]/[path]
```

with the components:

- `life` (key revision number) of the publisher's networking keys is used to identify which public key to use for signature verification.
- `path` is the actual user path in plaintext. This is not encrypted and is visible to all network observers.

Everything in the `%publ` namespace is public: both the publisher's identity/key version and the content path are visible to anyone. No encryption is applied to either the path or the message payload. Authentication comes solely from the Ed25519 signature, which proves the publisher created this content. Key rotation is supported through the life counter.

Its use cases include public data that should be readable by anyone, content where authenticity matters but confidentiality doesn't, and scenarios where simplicity is preferred over the complexity of encrypted namespaces (since no key exchange or group key distribution is required).

4.1.3 `%shut` namespace (group encrypted)

In contrast, the `%shut` namespace is intended for one-to-many encrypted data sharing, wherein a publisher ship shares data with a group of ships by encrypting the data with a shared symmetric key known to the group. The message is encrypted with XChaCha8 using this group symmetric key. The key is provided via the `%keen` task (not derived from ECDH). The encrypted path indicates which group key to use. Signature authentication takes place using a 64-byte Ed25519 signature computed over the encoded beam path and the LSS root of the encrypted data. The signature uses the publisher's Ed25519 private key, proving that the publisher created this encrypted payload. The receiver verifies the signature using the publisher's Ed25519 public key from Azimuth, then decrypts with the group key. In this security model, the signature proves authenticity from the publisher, while encryption provides confidentiality to group members. Anyone with the group key can decrypt, but only the publisher can create valid signatures.

The `%shut` namespace uses encrypted paths with the structure:

```
/shut/[key-id]/[encrypted-path]
```

with the components:

- `key-id`: A numeric identifier indicating which group symmetric key to use for decryption. This allows multiple groups to be supported, each with their own key.
- `encrypted-path`: The actual user path, encrypted using the group key. This is sealed with the same symmetric key used to encrypt the message payload, making the entire scry path opaque to anyone without the group key.

The actual content path is hidden from network observers. Only the key ID is visible in plaintext. The group key must be obtained separately (typically via a `%keen` task) to decrypt both the path and the message payload. Different groups using different key IDs can coexist without revealing which content is being accessed.

4.1.4 `%chum` namespace (1-to-1 encrypted)

The `%chum` namespace is intended for one-to-one encrypted data sharing between two ships. Authentication utilizes HMAC only (without signatures). The message is encrypted with XChaCha8 using a symmetric key derived from Curve25519 ECDH key exchange between the two ships' networking keys. A 16-byte HMAC (BLAKE3 keyed hash) is computed over the encoded beam path and the LSS root of the encrypted data, using the same ECDH-derived symmetric key. Both parties can independently derive this key from their own private key and the other party's public key. The receiver verifies the HMAC using the shared symmetric key, then decrypts with the same key. In this security model, the HMAC proves the sender possesses the shared symmetric key (implicitly authenticating them as the expected peer). No signatures are needed since only two parties share this key. This applies to both pokes and acks.

The `%chum` namespace uses encrypted paths with structure:

```
/chum/[server-life]/[client-ship]/[client-life]/
  [encrypted-path]
```

with the components:

- `server-life`: The life (key revision number) of the server ship's networking keys, used to identify which version of their keys to use for ECDH key derivation.

- `client-ship`: The `@p` address of the client ship in the communication pair.

- `client-life`: The life of the client ship's networking keys, used to identify which version of their keys to use for ECDH key derivation.

- `encrypted-path`: The actual user path, encrypted using the symmetric ECDH key derived from both ships' networking keys. This makes the scry path opaque to network observers.

This arrangement yields some nice privacy properties. The actual content path is hidden from network observers. Only the identities of both parties and their key versions are visible in plaintext. Only the two ships involved can derive the symmetric key to decrypt the path and payload. Key rotation is supported through the life counters.

4.1.5 Other Cryptographic Properties

Directed Messaging relies on the ability to rotate keys on chain for its forward secrecy. Future versions of the protocol might add a ratchet to minimize the damage if a private key is compromised.

4.2 Packet Authentication

One of the goals of Directed Messaging was to improve upon the safe but dumb conservative design of old Ames to sign every 1 KiB packet. The standard approach is to use asymmetric crypto to establish a shared AEAD key, and use it to authenticate each packet. This is just as safe as signing every packet, and orders of magnitude faster. However, one still can't verify that a peer is sending *correct* data until one has received the entire message. The remote could send 999 good packets and one bad, and the receiver has no way of knowing which was which. This is especially annoying if one wants to download in parallel from multiple peers: if the final result is invalid, which peer is to blame?

Verifying that a packet belongs to a particular message is a job for a Merkle tree. Thus the protocol needs to split message data into the leaves of a tree, and send both leaf data and tree hashes. Early on, we debated whether to make these distinct request types; we settled on interleaving them. Now the question becomes: which tree hashes does one need to send, and when does one send them?

The relevant design constraints were:

1. Sufficiently-small messages should not require more than one packet.
2. It should be possible to download in parallel.
3. The protocol should be flexible with respect to the size of a leaf.

An obvious first place to look for inspiration was Bao (O'Connor, 2018). However, Bao is not very amenable to being split into fixed-size packets: it intermingles leaf data and tree hashes into one stream, and the number of consecutive hashes varies based on the offset. You could modify it such that each packet consists of a leaf followed by at most one hash; indeed, this was the initial plan. Visually:

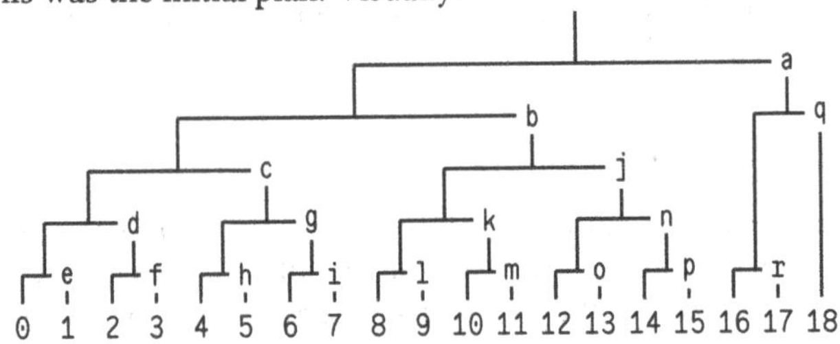

This is a binary numeral tree: a structure composed of perfect binary trees, imposed upon a flat sequence of bytes. The numbers 0–18 represent leaf data (typically 1 KiB per leaf), while letters `a`–`r` represents tree hashes that are used to verify the leaves. So packet 3 would contain bytes 3072–4096 and leaf hash `d`.

The main problem with this approach is that it requires buffering. In order to verify leaf 0, we need hashes `a` through `e` – five packets! Worse, once we've received five packets, we have the whole `[0,4)` subtree, making hashes `d` and `e` redundant. (In BNTs, we use the notation `[n,m)` to refer to the perfect subtree containing leaves `n` through `m-1`.)

Buffering a few packets is not the end of the world, but the whole thing had kind of a bad smell to it. We asked: what would happen if we added another constraint?

4. It should be possible to validate each packet as soon as it arrives, with no buffering.

For starters, an inescapable consequence of this constraint is that we must send the *full* Merkle proof for the first leaf before we can send the leaf data itself. Also, we can no longer send hashes that can't be immediately verified. For example, to verify `g`, we first need to have verified `c`; we can then combine `g` with its sibling hash and confirm that the result matches `c`.

While adding another constraint seems like it would make our life harder, in reality the opposite happened: the protocol was greatly simplified. It turns out that by front-loading the initial proof hashes, we ensure that the received leaf data and hashes will never "run ahead" of what can be immediately verified. Here's what it looks like in practice:

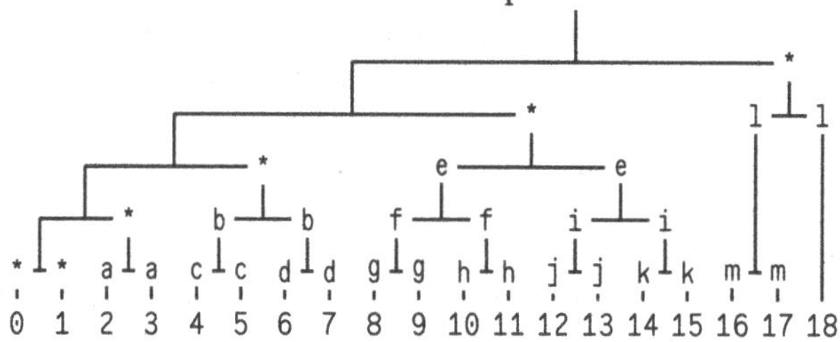

In the initial packet, we send the Merkle proof for leaf 0, i. e. all of the hashes marked with `*`. Each subsequent packet contains leaf data (leaf 0, 1, 2, etc.), and possibly a "pair" (`a`, `b`, `c`, etc.), which comprises *both* child hashes under a particular node. Packet-by-packet, the verifier sees:

```
Packet 0: Signed Merkle root + Merkle proof for leaf 0.
          Verify proof against signed root.
          We now have [0,1), [1,2), [2,4), [4,8), [8,16),
     and [16,19).
Packet 1: Leaf 0 + Pair a.
          Verify leaf 0 against [0,1).
          Verify pair a against [2,4).
          We now have [1,2), [2,3), [3,4), [4,8), [8,16),
     and [16,19).
Packet 2: Leaf 1 + Pair b.
          Verify leaf 1 against [1,2).
          Verify pair b against [4,8).
          We now have [2,3), [3,4), [4,6), [6,8), [8,16),
     and [16,19).
Packet 3: Leaf 2 + Pair c.
          Verify leaf 2 against [2,3).
          Verify pair c against [4,6).
          We now have [3,4), [4,5), [5,6), [6,8), [8,16),
     and [16,19).
... and so on.
```

At each step, we "consume" two hashes (one to verify a leaf, one to verify a pair), and add the pair to our verified set; thus, the number of verified-but-unused hashes stays constant until we get to packet 13. At this point, packets still contain leaf data (so we'll consume one hash), but there are no more pairs left to send; thus, our stockpile of hashes is steadily exhausted, until we consume the final hash to verify the final packet.

This is a solid improvement! We dubbed it "Lockstep Streaming," after the fact that verification proceeds in lockstep with packet receipt. But when we sat down to write the code for matching verified-but-unused hashes to incoming leaves and pairs, things got hairy. It was clearly *possible*, but the ugliness of the logic suggested that there was a better way. And after filling plenty of notebook pages with hand-drawn Merkle trees, `~rovnys-ricfer` found it: a mapping of packet numbers to hash pairs that was not only much cleaner, but also *scale invariant*. It's called Blackman ordering, and it looks like this:

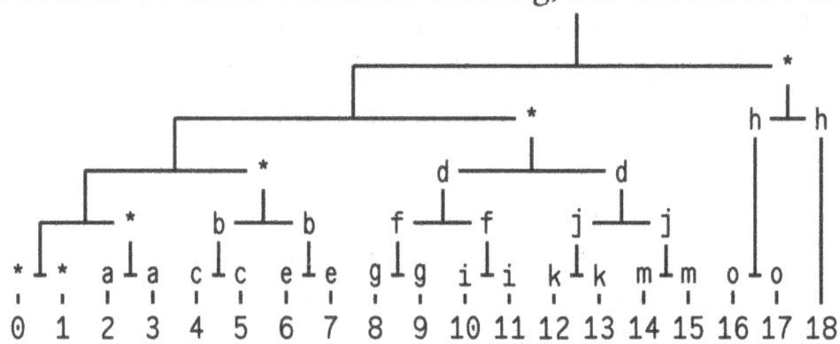

See the difference? Instead of ordering the pairs on a first-needed basis, we jump around a bit. Specifically, we send a pair whose "height" corresponds to the number of trailing zeroes in the binary representation of the packet number. For example, packet 4 is `0b100` in binary, with two trailing zeroes, so we send pair d, which sits two levels above the leaves.[3] Here is a packet-by-packet verification for Blackman ordering:

The `[x,y)` notation indicates a half-open set, i. e. it includes `x`, `x+1`, `x+2`, ..., `y-1`. `[2,4)` contains elements `2` and `3`. `[0,1)` contains the single element `0`.

```
Packet 0: Signed Merkle root + Merkle proof for leaf 0.
          Verify proof against signed root.
          We now have [0,1), [1,2), [2,4), [4,8), [8,16),
     and [16,19).
```

[3]As you might expect, the logic gets slightly less clean when the number of leaves is not a power of two, but it's hardly catastrophic.

```
Packet 1: Leaf 0 + Pair a.
          Verify leaf 0 against [0,1).
          Verify pair a against [2,4).
          We now have [1,2), [2,3), [3,4), [4,8), [8,16),
     and [16,19).
Packet 2: Leaf 1 + Pair b.
          Verify leaf 1 against [1,2).
          Verify pair b against [4,8).
          We now have [2,3), [3,4), [4,6), [6,8), [8,16),
     and [16,19).
Packet 3: Leaf 2 + Pair c.
          Verify leaf 2 against [2,3).
          Verify pair c against [4,6).
          We now have [3,4), [4,5), [5,6), [6,8), [8,16),
     and [16,19).
... and so on.
```

Shortly after, `~watter-parter` tweaked the ordering slightly, offsetting it by one; this further simplified the low-level bithacking. We called this variant "Lackman ordering," and it is used in the final version of Lockstep Streaming. A diagram of the order is depicted in Figure 2.

Per-packet verification for Lackman ordering looks like:

```
Packet 0: Signed Merkle root + Merkle proof for leaf 0.
          Verify proof against signed root.
          We now have [0,1), [1,2), [2,4), [4,8), [8,16),
     and [16,19).
Packet 1: Leaf 0 (no pair).
          Verify leaf 0 against [0,1).
          We now have [1,2), [2,4), [4,8), [8,16), and
     [16,19).
Packet 2: Leaf 1 + Pair a.
          Verify leaf 1 against [1,2).
          Verify pair a against [2,4).
          We now have [2,3), [3,4), [4,8), [8,16), and
     [16,19).
Packet 3: Leaf 2 + Pair b.
          Verify leaf 2 against [2,3).
          Verify pair b against [4,8).
          We now have [3,4), [4,6), [6,8), [8,16), and
     [16,19).
... and so on.
```

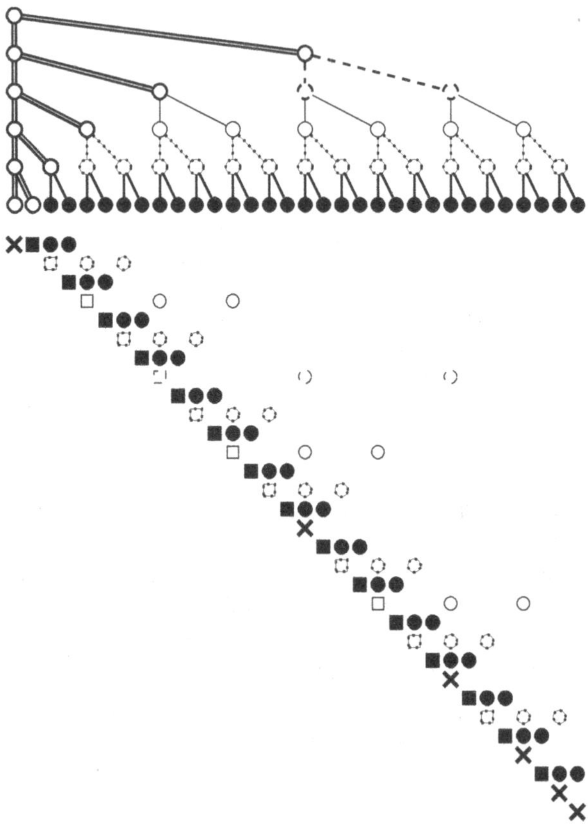

Figure 2: Lackman-ordered traversal. See Figure 3 for a time series.

Compared to Blackman ordering, the pairs appear offset by one position, which simplifies the bit-manipulation logic for computing which pair to include in each packet.

There's one more optimization worth mentioning: If the message is small enough, we can skip the initial step of sending a packet containing only a Merkle proof (with no leaf data). Obviously, for a one-leaf message, we can simply send that leaf; the hash of that leaf is the Merkle root. For a two-leaf message, we can send the leaf plus its sibling hash (`[1, 2]`); the verifier

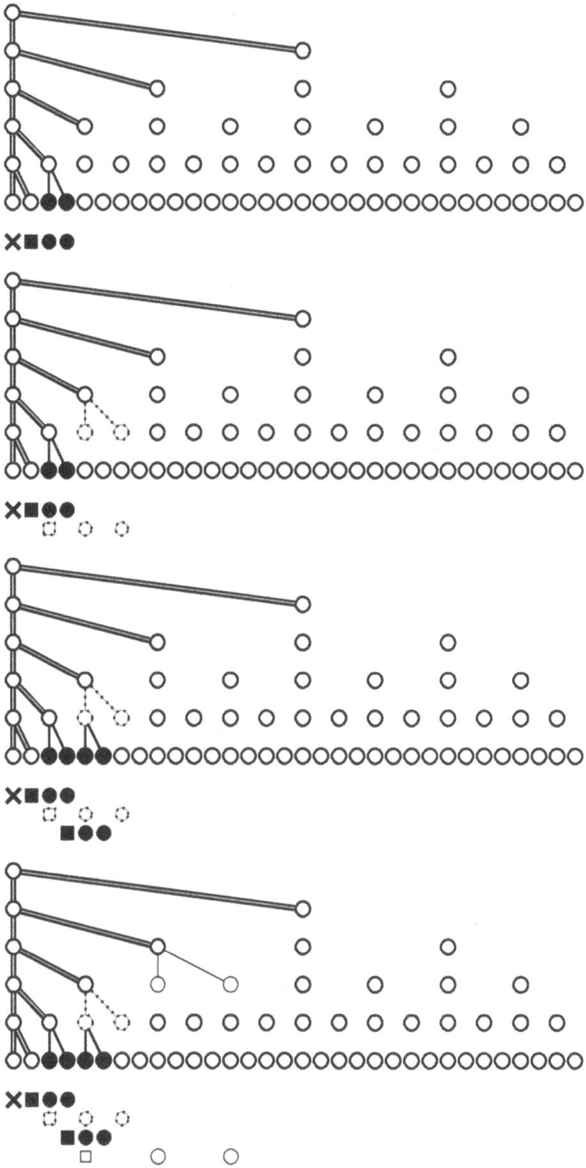

Figure 3: Lackman-ordered traversal as time series.

can hash the first leaf and combine it with the sibling hash to recover the root. And for a three- or four-leaf message, we can send `[1,2)` and `[2,3)` (or `[2,4)`, respectively). That's the limit, though; if a message has five leaves, we would need to send at least three sibling hashes for the verifier to recompute the root, but our packet framing only allows up to two hashes.

4.2.1 Arena Allocator

Directed Messaging uses a simple bump allocator arena for memory management. Each arena is a contiguous block of memory with three pointers: the start of the allocation (`dat`), the current allocation position (`beg`), and the end of the block (`end`). The `new()` macro allocates objects by advancing the `beg` pointer with proper alignment.

The arena allocator provides *no individual deallocation* – once memory is allocated from an arena, it can't be freed separately. Instead, the entire arena is freed at once when the data structure that owns it is destroyed.

Allocation Patterns Arenas are created with sizes tailored to their use case:

- **Pending Interest Table entries** use 16 KiB arenas. These store lane addresses for pending requests, with the arena holding the entry itself plus a linked list of address records.
- **Pending requests** allocate arenas at 5× the expected message size. A request receiving a 1 MiB message gets a 5 MiB arena. This single arena holds the request state, fragment data buffer, LSS authentication pairs, packet statistics, bitset tracking received fragments, and pre-serialized request packets.
- **Jumbo frame cache entries** allocate based on proof size, data size, hash pairs, plus a 2 KiB buffer. For a 1 MiB message, this might be around 1–2 MiB. The arena stores the cached response data, Merkle proof spine, and authentication hashes.

- **Temporary arenas** for packet sending use message size plus 16 KiB to hold serialized packets plus overhead.
- **Scry callbacks** get small arenas for asynchronous Arvo interactions.

Deallocation Triggers Arenas are freed only when their parent data structure is destroyed:

- **Request completion**: When all fragments arrive, the request is deleted and its arena freed. This happens asynchronously through `libuv`'s handle cleanup to ensure proper timer shutdown before freeing memory.
- **Authentication failure**: If LSS verification fails while processing fragments, the entire request is immediately deleted.
- **Timeout expiration**: When retry timers exhaust their attempts, the request is deleted.
- **PIT expiration**: After 20 seconds, entries are cleaned from the Pending Interest Table.
- **Cache eviction**: When the jumbo cache exceeds 200 MiB, it's entirely cleared and all cached arenas are freed.

Lifecycle A typical request lifecycle:

1. **Allocation**: Receive initial packet, create arena with 5× data size, allocate all request state from arena.
2. **Growth**: As fragments arrive, write into pre-allocated buffers within the arena.
3. **Completion**: All fragments received, construct final message, send to Arvo.
4. **Cleanup**: Delete request from map, stop timer, close handle asynchronously.

5. **Deallocation**: In UV callback, free entire arena with single call.

This design trades memory efficiency for speed. Arenas may hold unused space, but allocation is extremely fast (just pointer arithmetic), and the single-free design eliminates per-object deallocation overhead and fragmentation issues.

4.2.2 Download Checkpointing

This has not been deployed to the network, but this design allows the requesting ship's runtime to inject jumbo frames of arbitrary size into its Arvo as each one finishes downloading, with real authentication by using Lockstep. Arvo will seamlessly store those jumbo frames and accumulate them until it has the whole message, at which time it will deserialize the message into an Urbit 'noun' data structure and deliver it to the application or kernel module that had triggered the request.

This allows the system to make effective use of Arvo as a download checkpointing system. After a process crash, machine restart, or any other transient failure, the download can be resumed with minimal loss of information.

Injecting an authenticated jumbo frame into Arvo maintains a security boundary. Urbit's main runtime, Vere, has two Unix processes: one runs the Arvo kernel, and the other handles input and output. Arvo maintains ultimate responsibility for cryptographic operations. This lets the private key remain solely in the Arvo process, leaving the I/O process without the ability to encrypt, decrypt, authenticate, or verify authentication.

Instead, the runtime delegates any operation requiring a private key to Arvo, including validating the message-level authentication in the first packet of a scry response. To add a layer of defense in depth in case the I/O process is compromised, Arvo performs its own packet validation, including the Lockstep packet authentication. This remains efficient because each packet can be a large jumbo frame.

Checkpointing has another benefit. No matter how large a message is, the downloader can keep a fixed upper bound on the memory footprint while download that message, proportional to one jumbo frame.

4.2.3 Download Resumption

After a transient failure – most commonly a process crash or machine restart – a requesting ship can resume a download. In order to pick up from where it left off, the runtime first asks its local Arvo for the leaf-packet hashes it needs, which Arvo generates on demand from the jumbo frames that have already been downloaded and stored in Arvo. This is $O(\log(n))$ hashes, where n is the message length, and no message data needs to be sent over inter-process communication in order to resume a download, preventing restarts from becoming slow and memory-intensive.

Once the runtime has the hashes it needs, it resumes the Lockstep streaming verification that it had been doing, beginning with the next jumbo frame after the last one that had been downloaded and saved in Arvo.

Download checkpointing and resumption together provide a good set of tools for download management. This is beyond what TCP provides, or even HTTP. HTTP has resumption headers, but both client and server have to opt into using them, so in practice many HTTP-based downloads cannot be resumed.

5 Congestion Control

In Directed Messaging, congestion control is pluggable. The requesting ship decides how many request packets to send and at what time. The publisher ship is only responsible for responding to requests and does not participate in congestion control.

It is possible for an Urbit implementation to have functioning, if not performant, networking, without any runtime implementation of congestion control. The formal specification in the networking module of the Arvo kernel for how a ship sends request packets is a simple one-at-a-time indefinite repeating timer. The ship sends the first request packet, repeating it every thirty seconds until a response packet is heard, at which point it begins requesting the next packet.

Performant congestion control, then, is an extension of Urbit's idea of a "jet", i. e. a peephole optimization that replaces a built-in function, defined formally but is likely slow, with an optimized low-level implementation.

In practice, this slow packet re-send is used for retrying dead connections, where the publishing ship has been unresponsive for a long time. This is important because Urbit network requests generally do not time out at the application level; they are considered persistent, and they must be retried indefinitely. Fast, runtime-based congestion control only kicks in when the runtime receives a response packet, indicating the publishing ship has become responsive.

The current implementation of Directed Messaging employs a modified TCP Tahoe-style congestion control algorithm adapted to its request/response architecture and packet-oriented nature. The protocol's congestion control differs from traditional TCP in several fundamental ways due to its pull-based communication model and implicit acknowledgment scheme.

5.1 Architectural Foundation

Unlike TCP's push-based model where senders transmit data and await separate acknowledgment packets, Directed Messaging operates on a request/response paradigm. The requesting ship sends PEEK packets to solicit specific fragments, and the responding ship sends PAGE packets containing the requested data. The arrival of each PAGE packet serves as an implicit acknowledgment – no separate ACK packets exist in the protocol. This inversion places congestion control responsibility on the requester rather than the sender, allowing the party pulling data to directly regulate network load.

The protocol operates on fixed-size fragments rather than byte streams. Each fragment contains up to 1024 bytes of payload data (at the default `$bloq` parameter of 13). The congestion window (`cwnd`) measures capacity in fragment count rather than bytes, providing coarser but simpler granularity than TCP's byte-oriented approach.

5.2 State Variables

Congestion control state is maintained per peer and includes:

- `cwnd` (congestion window): Number of fragments allowed in flight simultaneously.
- `ssthresh` (slow start threshold): Boundary between exponential and linear growth phases.
- `rttvar` (RTT variance): Smoothed variance in round-trip measurements.
- `rto` (retransmission timeout): Calculated timeout for loss detection.

Per-request state tracks which fragments have been sent, when they were sent, how many retransmission attempts have occurred, and which fragments have been received using an efficient bitset representation.

5.3 Slow Start and Congestion Avoidance

The protocol implements two growth phases analogous to TCP:

- **Slow Start Phase** (`cwnd < ssthresh`): Upon initiating a request or recovering from congestion, `cwnd` begins at one fragment. For each fragment acknowledgment received (implicitly, by receiving the corresponding PAGE packet), `cwnd` increments by 1. This produces exponential growth: 1→2→4→8→16, allowing rapid probing of available bandwidth.
- **Congestion Avoidance Phase** (`cwnd >= ssthresh`): Once `cwnd` reaches `ssthresh`, growth becomes linear. The implementation uses a fractional accumulation strategy: for each acknowledgment, a fractional counter accumulates `1/cwnd` of a window increment. When the accumulated value reaches `cwnd`, the actual `cwnd` increments by 1, yielding approximately one window size increase per round-trip time.

The default `ssthresh` is initialized to 10,000 fragments (approximately 10 MiB), effectively allowing slow start to dominate for typical transfer sizes.

5.4 Loss Detection and Recovery

Directed Messaging currently implements timeout-based loss detection only, without fast retransmit or fast recovery mechanisms. This places it closest to TCP Tahoe's behavior, though with an important modification to timeout handling.

- **Timeout Detection**: Each in-flight fragment's transmission time is recorded. A retransmission timer fires when the oldest unacknowledged fragment exceeds the calculated RTO. The protocol scans all in-flight fragments upon timeout and retransmits any that have been outstanding beyond the RTO interval.
- **Timeout Response**: Upon detecting packet loss via timeout, the protocol reduces network load by:
    1. Setting `ssthresh = max(1, cwnd / 2)`.
    2. Setting `cwnd = ssthresh`.
    3. Doubling `rto` (up to a maximum bound).

This differs from TCP Tahoe, which sets `cwnd = 1` and restarts slow start from the beginning. Directed Messaging's approach is less conservative, immediately resuming transmission at the reduced threshold rather than slowly ramping up from a single packet. This assumes that while congestion occurred, the network can still sustain traffic at half the previous rate without requiring a full slow start restart.

The lack of fast retransmit (triggering on three duplicate acknowledgments) represents a significant difference from modern TCP variants. Fast retransmit requires detecting duplicate acks, which in Directed Messaging would mean detecting requests for the same fragment. However, the current implementation treats each arriving PAGE packet independently without tracking the ordering implications that would enable fast retransmit. This is a known simplification intended for future enhancement.

5.5 Round-Trip Time Estimation

The protocol employs Jacobson/Karels RTT estimation, the same algorithm used in TCP. When a fragment acknowledgment arrives (excluding retransmissions), the round-trip time measurement (`rtt_datum`) is calculated as the difference between current time and transmission time.

RTT smoothing uses exponential weighted moving averages with traditional TCP parameters:

- `rtt = (rtt_datum + 7*rtt) / 8`, $\alpha = 1/8$.
- `rttvar = (|rtt_datum - rtt| + 7*rttvar) / 8`, $\beta = 1/4$.
- `rto = rtt + 4*rttvar`.

The retransmission timeout `rto` is furthermore clamped to a minimum of 200 milliseconds and a maximum that varies by context (typically 2 minutes for most traffic, 25 seconds for keepalive probes to sponsors).

Retransmitted fragments do not contribute to RTT estimation, following Karn's algorithm to avoid ambiguity about which transmission is being acknowledged.

5.6 Selective Request Architecture

The implicit acknowledgment scheme combines naturally with selective fragment requesting. The protocol maintains a bitset tracking which fragments have been received. When requesting additional fragments during congestion-controlled transmission, the requester consults both the congestion window (how many new requests can be sent) and the bitset (which fragments are needed). This provides the benefits of TCP SACK without requiring additional protocol machinery – selectivity is inherent to the request/response model.

When fragments arrive out of order, the LSS (Lockstep Signature Scheme) authentication requires buffering misordered packets until their Merkle proof predecessors arrive. Once authenticated, these fragments are marked received in the bitset, and the congestion control state updates accordingly.

5.7 Request Rate Limiting

The congestion window limits the number of PEEK requests in flight. Before sending additional requests, the protocol calculates

```
available_window = cwnd - outstanding_requests
```

where `outstanding_requests` counts fragments that have been requested but not yet received. This naturally throttles the request rate according to observed network capacity. As PAGE packets arrive (serving as acknowledgments), `outstanding_requests` decreases, allowing new PEEK packets to be sent.

This pull-based flow control provides inherent advantages: the requester cannot be overwhelmed by data it didn't request, and the congestion control directly limits the rate at which the requester pulls data from the network.

5.8 Per-Peer State Management

Congestion control state is maintained per peer rather than per connection or per flow. All concurrent requests to the same peer share a single congestion window and RTT estimate. This design choice reflects the architectural principle that network capacity constraints exist between pairs of ships rather than between individual conversations.

Sharing state across requests to the same peer provides several benefits:

1. RTT measurements from any request improve estimates for all requests.
2. Congestion signals from one request protect other concurrent requests.
3. State initialization costs are amortized across multiple requests.
4. The aggregate transmission rate to each peer is controlled.

However, this also means that multiple concurrent large transfers to the same peer must share available bandwidth, which could reduce throughput compared to per-flow windows in some scenarios.

5.9 Initial Window and Probing

New peer connections begin with conservative initial values: `cwnd = 1`, `rtt = 1.000` ms, `rttvar = 1.000` ms, `rto = 200` ms.[4] The first fragment request initiates RTT measurement and slow start growth. This cautious initialization ensures the protocol probes network capacity gradually rather than assuming high bandwidth is available.

For peers with no recent traffic, the congestion state persists but becomes stale. Future enhancements may include state expiration and re-initialization after prolonged idle periods, though the current implementation maintains state indefinitely once a peer is known.

5.10 Comparison with TCP Variants

The congestion control algorithm most closely resembles TCP Tahoe but with notable differences:

Similarities to Tahoe:

- Slow start with exponential growth
- Congestion avoidance with linear growth
- Loss detection via timeout only
- Conservative initial probing

Differences from Tahoe:

- Modified timeout recovery (`cwnd = ssthresh` rather than `cwnd = 1`)
- Packet-oriented rather than byte-oriented windows

[4]Hoon atoms are written German-style, thus `1.000` for "one thousand".

- Implicit acknowledgment via data receipt
- Pull-based rather than push-based architecture
- Per-peer rather than per-connection state

Compared to NewReno/SACK, the protocol lacks fast retransmit and fast recovery, making it less responsive to isolated packet loss. However, the selective request architecture provides the functional benefits of SACK naturally. The implicit acknowledgment scheme eliminates issues with ACK loss and compression that affect TCP.

5.11 Design Trade-offs

The congestion control design reflects several architectural trade-offs. Advantages include:

- Simpler than modern TCP variants (no fast recovery complexity).
- Natural selective acknowledgment through request/response model.
- Requester controls rate, preventing receiver overwhelm.
- No separate ACK channel to fail.
- Precise retransmission control with bitset tracking.

The limitations include:

- Lack of fast retransmit increases latency for isolated losses.
- Packet-oriented windows provide coarser bandwidth control.
- Per-peer state sharing may reduce throughput for concurrent flows.
- Modified timeout behavior is less studied than standard algorithms.

5.12 Future Enhancements

The protocol architecture supports several potential improvements without fundamental redesign. Fast retransmit could be implemented by tracking fragment request patterns and detecting when requests skip over missing fragments. Fast recovery could leverage the existing `ssthresh` calculation while avoiding the full slow start restart. Additional sophistication in RTT measurement could distinguish network delay from application processing time.

The current implementation represents a pragmatic balance between simplicity and effectiveness, providing reasonable congestion control while keeping the protocol accessible to implementation and formal verification.

6 Integration

In order to deploy Directed Messaging to Urbit's live network, the previous version of the protocol needed to remain operational, since there is no central authority that can force Urbit ships to update to a particular version. The developers further decided that each ship should be able to upgrade connections to peer ships one by one, and should be able to downgrade without data loss.

This was possible due to the persistent, transactional nature of both the previous and new versions of the protocol.

6.1 Ames Flows

The Arvo kernel has a concept of an Ames "flow", a directed connection between ships where the subscriber ship can send commands and the publisher ship can send responses, both as "commands" at the level of Directed Messaging.

The implementation of Directed Messaging maintained the interface to the rest of the system, without modification. Applications do not need to modify their code at all to make use of Directed Messaging.

7 Conclusion

Directed Messaging provides a secure, efficient, and robust mechanism for requesting and receiving large messages in the Urbit network. By leveraging Lockstep Streaming for packet authentication and a modified TCP-like congestion control algorithm, it achieves high throughput while maintaining data integrity and resilience to network conditions. The protocol's design reflects Urbit's architectural principles of pull-based communication, implicit acknowledgment, and per-peer state management.

In fact, Azimuth's design, particularly star-based routing, suggests that star relaying and star scry caching could further enhance Directed Messaging's performance and reliability in a future development cycle. Download checkpointing and resumption could be fully supported by relays, as well as a fast retransmit mechanism integrated into the congestion control algorithm. Support for the "sticky scry" mechanism (UIP-0100) and `%pine` scry-at-latest (UIP-0121) will eventually round out a full pub-sub system built on top of Directed Messaging.

Directed Messaging represents a significant advancement over previous messaging protocols in Urbit, enabling applications to reliably transfer large amounts of data across the decentralized network.

References

Aumasson, Jean-Philippe (2019). "Too Much Crypto." In: *IACR Cryptology ePrint Archive*. URL: `https://eprint.iacr.org/2019/1492` (visited on ~2025.11.17).

Cheshire, Stuart (1996) "It's the Latency, Stupid". URL: `https://www.stuartcheshire.org/rants/latency.html` (visited on ~2025.11.16).

O'Connor, Jack (2018) "Bao". URL: `https://github.com/oconnor663/bao` (visited on ~2025.11.23).

~sorreg-namtyv, Curtis Yarvin, Philip Monk ~wicdev-wisryt, Anton Dyudin ~fyr, and Raymond Pasco ~sigryn-habrex (2016). *Urbit: A Solid-State Interpreter.* Whitepaper. Tlon Corporation. URL: https://media.urbit.org/whitepaper.pdf (visited on ~2024.1.25).

~watter-parter, Luke Champine (2021). *Streaming Merkle Proofs within Binary Numeral Trees.* Cryptology ePrint Archive, Paper 2021/038. URL: https://eprint.iacr.org/2021/038.

SUB KN AN

Subject Knowledge Analysis

K. Afonin ~dozreg-toplud
Urbit Foundation

Abstract

Classic Nock execution sees all function calls evaluate code dynamically. In practice, most Nock call sites have statically known code products given the subject. Subject Knowledge Analysis (SKA) is a static analysis pass to construct a call graph and subject mask from a subject-formula pair. The call graph facilitates direct calls in the bytecode interpreter and compile-time jet matching. The mask determines if two subject-formula pairs are equivalent to enable reuse of analysis results. SKA unlocks ample Nock performance gains.

Contents

Urbit Systems Technical Journal III:1 (2026): 43–67.
Address author correspondence to ~dozreg-toplud.

1 Introduction

To date, the Nock combinator calculus or instruction set (depending on one's viewpoint) has been evaluated using either a tree-walking interpreter or a bytecode interpreter. The former has been found straightforward to implement but regrettably slow in practice. Following a suggestion by `~ritpub-sipsyl` to incorporate better information about what is known about the subject into the compilation process, Urbit engineers elaborated Subject Knowledge Analysis, or SKA. This static analysis pass is performed on a subject-formula pair, producing a call graph and a subject mask. The latter can be used to determine if two subject-formula pairs are equivalent, allowing the reuse of analysis results. The call graph can be used to introduce direct calls in the bytecode interpreter, as well as to perform compile-time jet matching. SKA unlocks ample gains in practical Nock performance, as well as enabling future optimizations and analyses.

2 Dynamism of Nock

The Nock 2 operator is one of the two opcodes that are used for Nock evaluation. From the Nock specification:

```
*[a 2 b c]            *[*[a b] *[a c]]
```

Put plainly, we evaluate two operands of Nock 2 against the given subject, then evaluate Nock with the product of the first operand as a subject, and the product of the second operand as a formula.

The compound Nock 9 operator is defined in terms of other Nock operators:

```
*[a 9 b c]            *[*[a c] 2 [0 1] 0 b]
```

Evaluation of the formula from the second operator yields a noun, from which a formula to be evaluated is pulled with Nock 0. That formula is then evaluated against that noun, which is often referred to as a "core".

Since Nock 9 is essentially a macro for Nock 2, we can focus our attention on Nock 2. This operator is equivalent to `eval` in other languages: execution of dynamically generated code. Unlike most languages, Nock does not have a notion of a static call, and *all* function calls are implemented in terms of `eval`. In practice, however, we can discover formula products `*[a c]` for almost all Nock 2 sites, given the subject.

Examples when we cannot do that, such as receiving code to evaluate over the wire, or from the outer virtualization context via Nock 12, or as a product of a complex expression where we cannot reliably execute it at compile time, are rare. In practice, these exceptions are limited to either evaluating dynamically-supplied code or running the Hoon compiler at run time, e.g. in vase mode.[1] For all other cases, e.g. Arvo, Gall agents, the subject's code contents do not often change and the result of static analysis is likely to be reused until a kernel upgrade or Gall agent upgrade respectively.

This static analysis procedure, dubbed "Subject Knowledge Analysis", is as follows: given a pair of a subject and a formula,

[1]See `~lagrev-nocfep`, USTJ vol. 2 iss. 1, pp. 131–153, for more information on vase mode.

we construct the call graph for all Nock 2 sites for which we have enough information, yielding call graph information and subject mask. A new subject-formula pair where the formula is equal to the analyzed formula, and the parts of the subject included in the mask are equal to the same parts from the previously analyzed subject, is considered to be equivalent. Consider analyzing the subject-formula pair:

```
[[dec 1] [%9 2 %10 [6 %0 3] %0 2]]
```

Then a pair `[[dec 2] [%9 2 %10 [6 %0 3] %0 2]]` is equivalent to the first one in terms of the call graph information: the different subnouns of the subject are never used as code by the $ arm of the `dec` core. A pair of a minimized subject and a formula thus constructs an object equivalent to a function in other languages, with the masked out parts of the subject being the function's arguments. Further in the text, we will refer to pairs (minimized subject)-formula as functions that we discovered during the analysis.

3 Motivation

In prior work on SKA by `~ritpub-sipsyl` and `~master-morzod`, the analysis was considered as a first step in compiling Nock to a static single assignment intermediary representation language (SSA IR) to introduce direct calls in Nock. In their absence, Nock registerization, or any kind of optimization/analysis for that matter is limited by the lack of knowledge about the call target and the call product: in the SSA IR example, we would not know which parts of a call's subject are actually used by the callee program.

For the current work, a simpler goal was set: the introduction of direct calls and compile-time jet matching in the Vere bytecode interpreter. Currently, the interpreter has to, first, look up a Nock bytecode program in the bytecode cache, and second, it has to dynamically perform a jet matching routine at each Nock 9 call site.[2] With SKA, the bytecode programs

[2]There has been ongoing work to ameliorate the situation, such as `~fodwyt-ragful`'s Nockets project.

could have instructions for direct calls into other bytecode programs, and a program could also check if a given Nock 2 site matches some jet information the program has already accumulated, thus adding the jet driver directly into the bytecode stream if the match was obtained.

4 Core Algorithm

To analyze a subject-formula pair, we run what is essentially a partial Nock interpreter to propagate known information to formulas deeper in the formula tree, and to accumulate call graph information. Instead of a noun, the subject is a partial noun described with the type `$sock`:

```
+$  cape  $~(| $@(? [cape cape]))
+$  sock  $~([| ~] [=cape data=*])
```

That is, `$cape` is a mask that describes the shape of the known parts of a given noun, and `$sock` is a pair of a mask and data, where unknown parts are stubbed with `0` or `~`.

The treatment of the partial noun by that interpreter is mostly trivial:

- Autocons conses the partial products, normalizing the mask and data if necessary.

- Nock 0 grabs a subnoun from `$sock` if it can, otherwise it returns unknown result `[| ~]`.

- Nock 1 returns a fully known result.

- Actual computations (Nock 3, Nock 4, and Nock 5) return unknown result `[| ~]` – we do not attempt to run all code at compile time, we just want to evaluate code-generating expressions.

- Nock 6 produces an intersection of the results of branches, that is, only parts of the products that are known and equal between branches.

- Nock 7 composes formulas: the product of the first formula is passed as a partial subject to the second one.

- Nock 10 edits the product of one formula with the product of the other. If the recipient noun is not known, and the donor noun is known at least partially, cells will be created that lead to the edited part.

- Nock 8 and Nock 9 are desugared in terms of Nock 7, Nock 2, and autocons.

- Nock 11 calls have their dynamic hint formula products dropped and some hints are handled directly.

  - `%spot` hints are used for debugging/verbose printouts.

  - `%fast` hints are used to accumulate cold state.

- Nock 12 of the virtual Nock produces an unknown result.

In the case of Nock 2, the operands are evaluated, and then we check if the formula at this site is fully known. If it is not known, the call is *indirect* – we cannot make any assumptions about its product, so we return `[| ~]`. If it is known, we do two things:

1. We record information on subject usage as code for each call below us in the stack, including the root call. This step is needed to produce a minimized subject for each call, which is necessary to avoid redoing the work for the functions we already analyzed.

2. We enter a new frame of the partial interpreter, executing/analyzing new `$sock`–formula pair we just got, returning the result of that analysis as a product.

To track the code usage of the subjects of function calls, the partial noun is paired with a structure to describe the flow of data from the functions below us in the stack to the new callsite. That data structure will be described later in the performance section.

5 Loop handling

The most complicated part of the algorithm is the handling of loops. Unlike the regular interpreter, where only one branch is executed at a time, the partial interpreter enters both, so a lack of loop handling would quickly lead to an infinite cycle in the analysis, be it a simple decrement loop or mutual recursion in the Hoon compiler.

5.1 Loop detection

One way to detect loops would be to simply compare `$sock`-formula pairs that we have on the stack with the one that we are about to evaluate. That, however, would not work with functions that, for example, recursively construct a list, as the subject `$sock` would change from iteration to iteration. So instead of a simple equality check, we need to see if the new subject (further referred to as *kid* subject, or subject of the *kid call*) nests under the subject of the supposedly matching function call on the stack (*parent* subject, or subject of the *parent call*), given the current information we have about the usage of parent subject as code.

The problem is that the code usage information for the parent is not complete until we analyzed all its callees/descendants. Therefore, that loop guess would have to be validated when we return from the loop, and before that, no analysis of function calls in that loop can be finalized. We can see that we have three kinds of function calls: ones that are not a part of any cycle, and can be finalized immediately, ones that are in the middle of a cycle and cannot be finalized unless the entry point into that cycle is finalized, and finally, those that are the entry points into a cycle, whose finalization also means finalizing all members of a cycle. Another interesting aspect is that we do not know which kind of a function call we have on entry, we know it only on return. For the non-finalizable calls, we also do not know which call finalization they depend on until that loop entry is finalized, since we could always discover a new loop call that points deeper into the stack.

5.2 Call graph topology

We first describe in more detail what an abstract call graph is and how it is traversed and discovered in SKA.

The call graph is a directed graph with the vertices being the functions and the edges being function calls. The graph has a root, which is the top-level function that is being analyzed. We include function calls from callers to callees, even if the calls are conditional: from the point of view of the call graph topology, conditional calls of functions B and C performed by a function A are indistinguishable from consecutive calls, i.e. these two Hoon expressions would yield the same call graph shape (but the other information could, of course, be different):

```
?:  condition
  (func-a x)
(func-b x)
::
(func-b (func-a x))
```

We can see that, when we execute Nock, we traverse the call graph in depth-first, head-first order, except we skip some edges if they are conditional. As we enter other functions, the path from the root vertex to the current one forms the computational stack.

The abstract call graph may contain cycles. Figure 1 shows the abstract call graph for Nock obtained from compiling `(dec 42)` against `..ride` subject. Firstly `dec` expression is evaluated, which pulls `+dec` arm from a core in the subject. With the product of that expression, which is the `dec` core, pinned to the subject, we edit that core with the argument `42`, then we pull the arm `$` from that core. The `$` arm call either returns the decremented value or calls itself, incrementing the counter.

When we traverse that call graph, we cannot simply follow the edge from `$:dec` to itself, as doing so would cause an infinite loop in the algorithm. Instead, when we detect a loop call, or a *backedge*, we immediately return an unknown result from the child call. As we traverse the call graph, we enumerate the vertices, as shown in Figure 2.

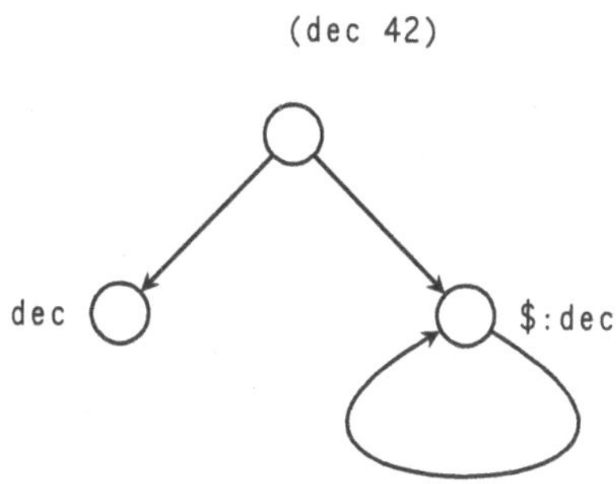

Figure 1: Abstract call graph for `(dec 42)`.

Figure 2 also demonstrates that the SKA representation of the call graph is acyclic: back-pointing edges are replaced with a forward-pointing edge to a new vertex that we do not analyze through. Together with the fact that both branches are traversed in Nock 6 analysis, SKA call graph traversal becomes a genuine depth-first, head-first traversal.

5.3 Loops as strongly connected components

From the point of view of the abstract, cyclical call graph, a set of functions that cannot be finalized unless all functions from this set are finalized forms a strongly-connected component (SCC) of that call graph. Thus, handling of loops in SKA becomes a question of handling SCCs. The algorithm that follows was developed by the author to detect and manage SCCs during the analysis. The process turned out to be quite similar to Tarjan's 1972 algorithm for finding SCCs with some differences:

- In Tarjan's algorithm, the graph is known ahead of time, while in SKA the graph is simultaneously inferred with symbolic execution of Nock and traversed.
- Since Nock call graph is rooted, only one traversal is necessary, and in this traversal the descendants down the

non-loop call edges are guaranteed to have higher index values.

The latter fact allows for simpler comparisons and simpler state management, allowing to have a stack of SCCs instead of a stack of vertices that are popped when an SCC is finalized. For example, when returning from a vertex which is a member of a non-trivial SCC in SKA we only have to check one boolean value and compare the index of this vertex with the index of the entry of the current SCC with equality operator, so we do not have to call arithmetic functions and pay Nock function call overhead.

As the call graph is traversed, we keep track of the stack of mutually independent SCCs (that is, SCCs whose unions are not SCCs) by keeping track of the entry point (the earliest vertex that has a backedge pointing to it) and the *latch* (the latest vertex that has a backedge originating from it).

Suppose that we encounter a new backedge. To determine whether it forms a new SCC, or belongs to an already existing one, it is sufficient to compare the parent vertex enumeration label with the latch of the latest SCC on the loop stack. If the parent vertex is greater than the latch, a new SCC data structure is pushed on the stack; otherwise, the top SCC's entry and latch are updated, and then that SCC is repeatedly merged with the one beneath it if the connection condition is satisfied: the entry of the updated SCC is less than or equal to the latch of the preceding SCC.

Let us prove that this comparison is sufficient. Recall that the enumeration labels are assigned in depth-first, head-first order. If the backedge parent is equal to the latch of the SCC, the kid is a part of the SCC since the kid is reachable by an SCC member, in this case, the parent, and a member of SCC is reachable from kid via the backedge (Figure 3).

If the parent label is greater than the latch, then either they are on the same root path or not. In both cases, no member of the SCC can be reached from the parent, making the parent, kid, and all vertices in between a new SCC. These scenarios are illustrated in Figure 4.

Finally, if the parent label is less than the latch, then either

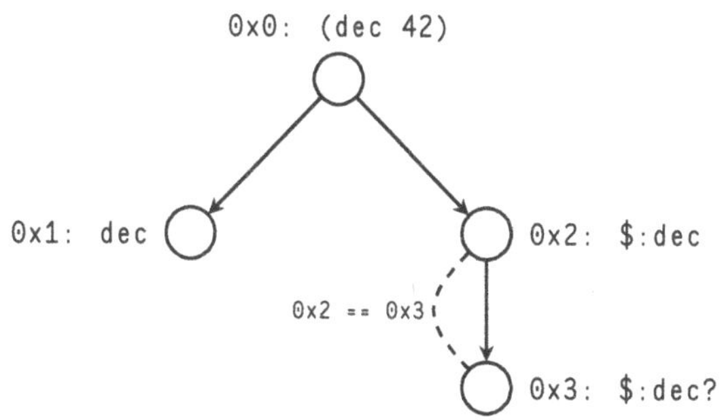

Figure 2: Call graph for `(dec 42)` in the middle of SKA. Vertices `0x2` and `0x3` form a loop (strongly connected component, SCC) with vertex `0x2` being the entry point (magenta), and vertex `0x3` being the latest (i.e. rightmost, deepest) vertex that belongs to that SCC, also called a *latch* of this SCC (orange). The dashed gray line denotes the loop assumptions that are to be validated upon exit from the SCC entry point. Vertex `0x3` is not analyzed through.

they are on the same root path or not.

If they are, the latch is the parent's descendant, making the latest SCC reachable from the parent. Since the parent and the kid are necessarily of the same root path, which makes the kid reachable from the latch, making both the parent and the kid vertices reachable from the SCC, thus making the kid, parent, and all vertices between them are part of the previous SCC.

If they are not, then the latch still has to be a parent's descendant. Let us sketch the proof by disproving the contrary.

Suppose that the opposite is true. Then the parent vertex is to the left of the latch, where "A is to the left of B" means that A is entered before B and A is not B's predecessor. The latch is either on the same root path as the kid or it is to the left of the kid vertex, since the latter is the latest vertex we discovered.

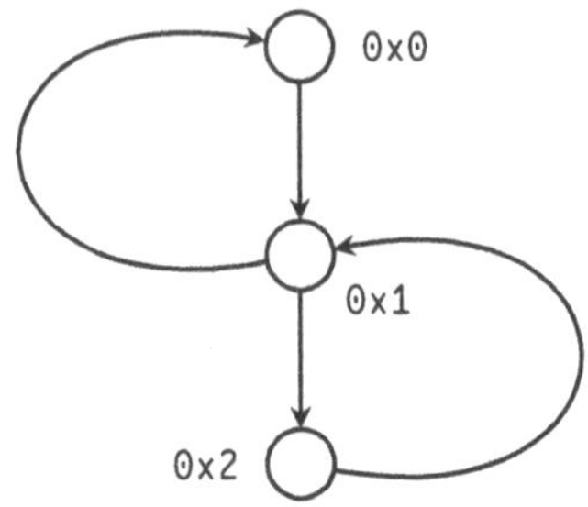

Figure 3: New backedge points to the latch of previous SCC, extending that SCC.

Since "leftness" is transitive, that means that the parent is to the left of the kid, which is impossible since they are on the same root path. Contradiction: the latch and the parent are on the same root path, making the kid, parent vertices, and vertices between them parts of the existing SCC. Illustrations for both scenarios are shown in Figure 5.

The condition for SCC merging in case of SCC extension is the same. In fact SCC extension can be represented in terms of SCC creation, together with merging with the topmost SCC in the loop stack.

5.4 Cycle Validation, Code Usage Distribution, Fixed-Point Search

Since loop validation is deferred until returning from the loop entry point, subject usage by the loop calls is not recorded until that point. At loop validation, we want to distribute subject code usage information of the parent over the kid's subject provenance, finally making an update we deferred so far. But by doing so, since the kid's subject may contain nouns from the parent call, given that the kid is always a parent's descendant in the call graph, we might update usage information of the parent's subject. We would have to do that in a loop until the parent's subject usage converged to the fixpoint value for that transformation.

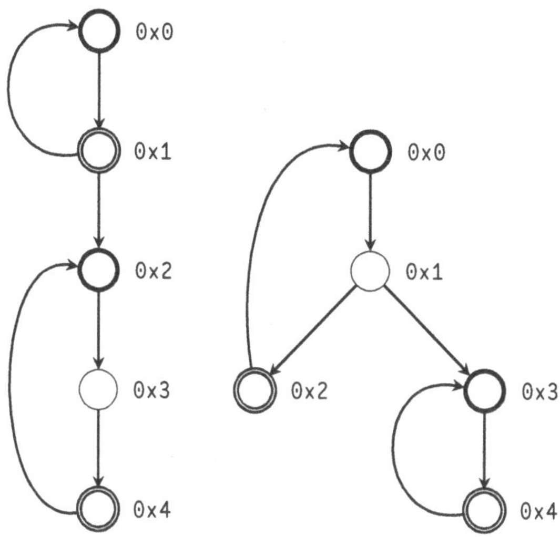

Figure 4: A new backedge points to a vertex with a label greater than the latch of the previous SCC, creating a new SCC with `0x2` as entry and `0x4` as latch on the left, and `0x3` as an entry and `0x4` as a latch on the right.

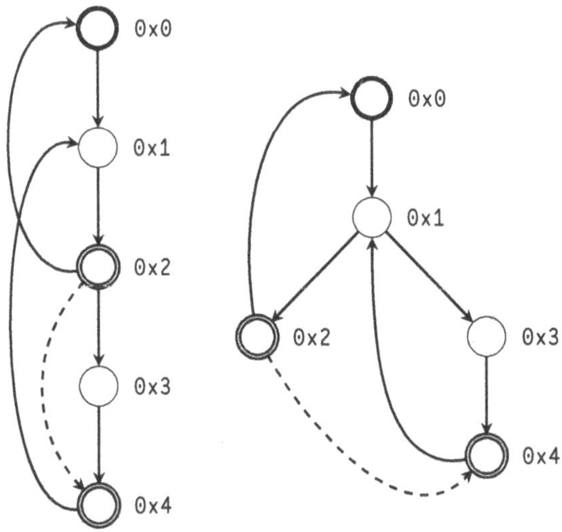

Figure 5: A new backedge points to a vertex with a label less than the latch of the previous SCC, extending that SCC and moving the latch to a new position.

For each backedge that we are validating, we perform the following steps:

1. We calculate the parent subject, masked down with the subject code usage information.
2. We distribute the `$cape` of that masked subject using kid provenance information.
3. We recalculate the new masked-down parent subject.
4. We compare their `$capes`. If they are equal, the fixpoint is found; otherwise, return to step 2.
5. Check masked-down parent subject and kid subject for nesting. If they nest, the backedge is valid; otherwise, the assumption was wrong, and we will redo the analysis of the loop with this parent-kid pair added to a blacklist.

Steps 1 and 3 are necessary because otherwise, if we distribute just the subject code usage information `$cape` without using it to mask actual data, the `$cape` could start growing infinitely deep, causing an infinite loop in the fixpoint search. Step 4 works because the `$cape` distribution along the given provenance is idempotent.

6 Performance: load-bearing design choices and optimizations

6.1 Vastness of nouns

It is important to have a sense of scale when dealing with SKA. Consider, for example, Urbit's standard library core `zuse`. How many nouns are there in total in that library? In Arvo 409K:

```
> =/  n=*  ..zuse
  |-  ^-  @
  ?@  n  1                        ::  atom is one noun
  ~+                              ::  %memo hint
  +((add $(n -.n) $(n +.n)))      ::  cell is 1 noun +
                                  ::   nouns in head +
                                  ::   nouns in tail
1.656.521.503.863.284.811.637
```

This yields 1.66×10^{21} nouns! "Billions of billions" would be an underestimate.

But Urbit's runtime, Vere, handles this mass of nouns just fine. We can estimate that it takes only about 1.2 MB to store that library. What is going on? And how can anything calculate the number of nouns in a reasonable time with something that looks like naive tree traversal?

The answer lies in structural sharing.[3] The standard library supplies many duplicated nouns, which are represented as pointers to reference-counted data structures. The reason we could count the number of nouns with something that seems

[3]See `~rovyns-ricfer` and `~wicdev-wisryt` in USTJ vol. 1 iss. 1, pp. 75–82, for details.

like a simple tree traversal is the use of `%memo` hint that enables memoization of Nock results, using the subject-formula pair as a key. Even if the nouns are large, their comparison is still fast precisely because they are duplicated: noun equality check is short-circuited on pointer equality. So even though pointer equality is not exposed in Nock directly, having nouns be pointer-equivalent is crucial for performance. Thus, when developing algorithms with performance in mind, we need to:

1. Make sure not to disrupt structural sharing whenever possible;

2. Leverage structural sharing by either short-circuiting various checks/comparisons with Nock 5 equality test, or by using Nock memoization.

6.2 Provenance Tree

We represent the provenance information of the subject with `$source`:

```
+$  source  (lest (lest *))
```

where `lest` is a non-empty list.

Raw nouns in the inner list describe the provenance from a function call's subject to a use site of that noun. The value can be one of:

- 0, if the noun does not come from the subject, e.g., it was created. by evaluating Nock 1 from the formula;

- a non-zero atom, in which case the noun comes from the given axis of the subject.

- a cell, in which case the noun in question is also a cell, and its head and tail have provenances that are described by the head and tail of the provenance noun respectively.

Nock 1, 3, 4, 5, and 12 erase provenance information. Nock 0 gets a sub-provenance tree in an obvious way. Nock 7 composes the provenance calculation. Nock 10 performs an edit.

All are similar to the `$sock` treatment. What differs significantly is the handling of the branching operator Nock 6. What we care about is where the data *could* come from, so we need to calculate a union of provenances, masked down to the intersection of produced data. Instead of creating a tree that includes all union information, in the spirit of saving structural sharing, we simply make a list of simple provenances. Thus `(lest *)` is a union of provenances in a given call.

The outer list keeps entries per call frame. Whenever we enter a new call with Nock 2, we push the new provenance union list `~[1]` onto the provenance stack. When we return from a call, the stack is popped, and the popped provenance union list is composed with the second-to-top. Whenever we need to distribute subject usage, e.g., when we encounter a direct call, the provenance stack is folded with composition.

6.3 Provenance tree operations and heuristics

When dealing with provenance information `$source`, some heuristics were added to improve performance. When applying binary functions like composition to two union lists of provenances, the function would be applied to all pairs, and a new union list would be constructed, omitting duplicates or other provenances that nest under some other provenance that is already present in the assembled list. The compatibility check function only checks provenance nouns up to ten cells deep, assuming that they are incompatible beyond that point. This heuristic prevents from walking provenance nouns exhaustively and taking too much time if they are too deep at the expense of possibly having larger union lists with duplicates, which does not affect the semantics of the algorithm. In case of Nock 10 provenance edit, the check was disabled altogether if the lengths of the union lists of donor and recipient nouns multiplied exceeded 100.

Since the provenance union is expressed as a list, there are two ways of implementing the consing of provenances. We can either cons every member of the list of the head provenance with every member of the list of the tail provenance, yielding a union list with the length equal to the product of the lengths of the operand lists. Alternatively, we can cons every member of the list of the head provenance with empty provenance `0`, cons `0` with every member of the list of the tail provenance, then concatenate the lists. That way, we end up with a union list whose length is a sum of the operand lists' lengths. The algorithm for consing chooses between two approaches depending on the length of the operand lists, using the multiplicative approach almost always, since typically the union list length is one, and switching to the additive "cons via union" if the union lists are too long.

6.4 Load-bearing comparison checks and `%memo` hints

In `$cape` and `$sock` arithmetic, equality check shortcuts for `$cape` union, which is heavily used for code usage information updates, and `$sock` intersection, which is used for Nock 6 product calculation, are load-bearing. For `%memo` hints, we use them to short-circuit Nock memoization hints, these are load-bearing for provenance noun composition and construction of subject capture mask used for in-algorithm caches described below. They also appear to add marginal performance improvements in other places of the algorithm in case of backtracking (reanalyzing a cycle over and over due to making incorrect guesses).

6.5 Algorithm caches for finalized and non-finalized calls

To prevent doing the same work over and over, we want to cache the intermediary analysis results. For finalized calls, the cached data includes the formula and the minimized subject, where the latter includes potential subject capture in addition to code usage. If a Nock 2 formula gets a cache hit, it updates the code usage information using the mask from the cache, and returns the product, which it constructs by taking the cached product `$sock` and composing the cached union list with current subject provenance, effectively applying the provenance transformation of the cached call to the new subject.

Caching finalized calls turned out to be not enough, as demonstrated by `~ritpub-sipsyl` and `~master-morzod`.[4] To prevent reanalysis of cycles in highly mutually-recursive code like the Hoon compiler, caching of non-finalized calls was also necessary. Similarly to finalized-call caching, a potential cache match would check the subject it has for nesting with the cached subject `$sock`, masked down at cache check time with the currently available code usage information. Similarly to loop calls, the code usage information distribution along the new subject provenance would be deferred to the cycle validation. Another point of similarity is the necessity of checking cycles for overlap and merging in case they do, since a cache hit call would have a loop call to a member of an SCC to which the cached function belongs.

Unlike loop calls, the fixpoint search is not necessary since the cached call and the cache hit are never on the same root path, so distributing the code usage information along the hit call subject provenance would never have an effect on cached call. Validation is still necessary, and reanalysis of cycles due to incorrect non-finalized call cache guesses is currently the biggest overhead in the analysis.

7 Vere integration

The integration of SKA analysis into Vere was done in the simplest imaginable way as a proof of concept. The road struct was updated to include bytecode caches for SKA-produced code and to house the analysis core. A new static hint `%ska` marks the entry point into the analysis-compilation lifecycle.

7.1 Nomm (Nock--)

In addition to producing call graph information, the SKA algorithm also produced desugared, annotated Nock-like code called Nomm (a sort of Nock--). The practical difference, apart

[4]See `~ritpub-sipsyl` and `~master-morzod`, "Subject Knowledge Analysis", Urbit Lake Summit, ~2024.6.19; at the time of press, a copy is available at `https://www.youtube.com/watch?v=Z4bX4n1JH8I`.

from Nock 9 and Nock 8 expanded into other Nock operators, is the annotation data in Nock 2. The version of Nomm that is provided for use with the Vere development fork with SKA, `$nomm-1`, is mostly indistinguishable from `$nock` proper:

```
+$  nomm-1
  $^  [nomm-1 nomm-1]
  $%  [%1 p=*]
      [%2 p=nomm-1 q=nomm-1 info=(unit [less=sock fol=*])]
      [%3 p=nomm-1]
      [%4 p=nomm-1]
      [%5 p=nomm-1 q=nomm-1]
      [%6 p=nomm-1 q=nomm-1 r=nomm-1]
      [%7 p=nomm-1 q=nomm-1]
      [%10 p=[p=@ q=nomm-1] q=nomm-1]
      [%11 p=$@(@ [p=@ q=nomm-1]) q=nomm-1]
      [%12 p=nomm-1 q=nomm-1]
      [%0 p=@]
  ==
```

In the case of `%2`, `info=~` denotes an indirect call, and a non-empty case denotes a direct call with a known formula and masked subject. The pair of a minimized subject and a formula is used here as a unique identifier for a Nomm function.

7.2 Road data structures

Two HAMT tables were added to the `u3a_road` struct: `dar_p`, a map from [sock formula] pair to loom offset of `u3n_prog` bytecode `u3p(u3n_prog)`, and `lar_p`, a map from formula to a list of pairs `[sock u3p(u3n_prog)]`. The former is used during Nomm compilation to bytecode, the latter is used for searching for bytecode with direct calls, given a formula and a subject.

The Nock bytecode struct was extended with an array of direct call information structs:

```
/* u3n_dire: direct call information
 */
typedef struct {
  u3p(u3n_prog)  pog_p;
  u3j_harm*      ham_u;
  c3_l           axe_l;
```

```
} u3n_dire;
```

where

- `pog_p` is a bytecode program loom offset for the direct call,
- `ham_u` is a nullable pointer to a jet driver if the jet match occurred at compile time,
- `axe_l` is the arm axis for jet driver debugging checks.

Another addition to the road struct was a field for the analysis core `+ka`. A jammed cell of four pre-parsed Hoon ASTs for SKA source files was added to Vere source code, which was unpacked and built into a core when the SKA entry point was executed with `+ka` core not being initialized.

7.3 Analysis lifecycle

Let us follow the execution of a [subject formula] pair using SKA. It starts with annotating a computation with a `%ska` hint:

```
~>  %ska
```

7.3.1 `%ska` hint

When the regular bytecode compiler in Vere encounters a `%ska` hint, it defers the compilation of the hinted formula and emits SKA-entry point opcode. When that opcode is executed, a lookup is performed in `lar_p`, returning `u3n_prog*` on success. If the lookup failed, the pair of subject and formula is passed to `+rout` gate of the `+ka` core, which returned `+ka` core with global code tables and cold state updated. After that, the code maps were extracted from the global state, and the SKA compiler function was called with the subject, formula, and the maps as arguments. The maps include:

- `cole`: a map from `[sock *]` to `[path axis]` for cold state accumulation,

- `code`: a map from `[sock *]` to loom offset of `u3n_prog` for finalized call caching,
- `fols`: a map from formula to a list of pairs `[sock u3p(u3n_prog)]` for non-finalized call caching.

7.3.2 Nomm compilation and execution

The main difference between compiling regular Nock to Vere bytecode and compiling Nomm is that compiling a Nomm formula with direct calls also requires compiling all its callees recursively. A rewrite step was added to handle cycles properly: on the first pass `u3_noun` values for `[sock *]` pairs were saved in `u3n_dire` structs, and on the second pass, these values were replaced with corresponding `u3p(u3n_prog)` values.

Once the bytecode program for the entry point function and all its descendants were compiled, the Nock bytecode interpreter would execute this program as any other program, with the only difference of having direct call opcodes that skip bytecode cache lookup and jet matching.

7.4 Benchmarks and Notable Results

The effect of the `%ska` hint on performance was compared for the Ackermann function and a simple list iteration algorithm. In both cases, the performance gain was around 1.7×. The main overhead in computations with direct calls appears to come from refcounting/ allocating/freeing operations and interpretation (Figures 6 and 7).

When it comes to the performance of the SKA algorithm itself, the results were sometimes surprising. Paradoxically, analyzing `+mint:ut` call itself took `~m1`, while analyzing the entirety of `hoon.hoon`, including `+mint:ut`, takes `~s13`. The reason appears to be a lack of knowledge in the solo `+mint:ut` call case, causing excessive backtracking due to wrong non-finalized call cache hits (thus validating SKA's fundamental thesis). In addition, every time the loop analysis was discarded, all caches were also discarded, leading to making more work multiple times when compared to the `hoon.hoon` case. In the latter case, no wrong cache hits were made.

Figure 6: Flame graph for Ackermann function computation without `%ska` hint.

Figure 7: Flame graph for Ackermann function computation with `%ska` hint.

8 Conclusion and future work

There appear to be two viable future directions for this project. A short-term objective is a proper integration with the Vere runtime, such as making compiled SKA bytecode caches persistent and integrating cold states of Vere and SKA. A longer-term direction would pursue `~ritpub-sipsyl`'s original vision by implementing SSA IR compilation, which would ameliorate allocation overhead caused by cell churning[5] during temporary core construction for calls and deconstruction to get function arguments.

References

Tarjan, Robert Endre (1972). "Depth-First Search and Linear Graph Algorithms." In: *SIAM Journal on Computing* 1.2, pp. 146–160. DOI: 10.1137/0201010. URL: https://epubs.siam.org/doi/10.1137/0201010.

[5]Compare the rationale for the implementation of the # hax edit instruction in Nock 4K as explained by `~fodwyt-ragful`. (See `~lagrev-nocfep` and `~sorreg-namtyv`, "A Documentary History of the Nock Combinator Calculus", *USTJ* vol. 2 iss. 1, pp. 75–82, for historical context.)

GW C C

Groundwire Comet Cryptography

Trent Steen ~hanfel-dovned
Groundwire Foundation

Abstract

This article presents three coordinated changes to comet identity and networking on Urbit:

1. Ames may query Jael for a comet's current life and networking keys instead of requiring comet self-attestation;
2. Introduction of a cryptosuite with tweaked signing keys, binding keys to explicit provenance data while preserving Suite B compatibility; and
3. Optional fief-based routing, allowing comets to route directly by static IP or domain and lifting the assumption that sponsor chains must terminate at galaxies.

Collectively, comet identity becomes cryptographically coupled to the chosen PKI substrate while remaining substrate-agnostic at the protocol level.

Adapted from UIP-0136.[1]

Contents

[1]The author would like to thank ~tinnus-napbus and ~bonbud-macryg for help documenting the original Groundwire codebase, and ~tondes-sitrym and ~sarpen-laplux for developing it.

Urbit Systems Technical Journal III:1 (2026): 69–82.
Address author correspondence to ~hanfel-dovned.

1 Introduction

Urbit currently derives comet identity from self-attested networking keys whose public half hashes into the comet's `@p`. In practice, this creates an implicit coupling between a comet's keys and whichever source of truth a peer happens to trust at first contact.

Groundwire's proposal is deliberately modest and pragmatic. Over the long term, we believe Bitcoin is the only chain that defines canonical history at the protocol level (the heaviest valid proof-of-work chain) in a way that a zero-kelvin Urbit could verify without social coordination or trusted checkpoints. This makes Bitcoin an attractive long-term anchor for the Urbit PKI. At the same time, it is premature to elevate that belief to kernel policy or to bless a single on-chain abstraction (e.g., ordinals/inscriptions) in perpetuity. Different chains—and even different protocols on the same chain—offer distinct data and scripting affordances for identity; we should let those options be explored in the field.

Accordingly, we propose a substrate-agnostic mechanism whereby:

- Ames first consults Jael for comet keys and only falls back to comet self-attestation if Jael lacks a record.
- Networking keys may be *tweaked* using explicit provenance data, so the key material itself cryptographically commits to the on-chain (or off-chain) attestation it corresponds to.

- Comets may advertise routing information (a `$fief`) so packets can route directly without assuming a sponsorship hierarchy that must terminate at galaxies.

This leaves the memorable-name hierarchy (galaxies, stars, planets) on Azimuth untouched while upgrading the vast expanse of ephemeral identities for self-sovereign networking. Practically, Jael continues to subscribe to sources (via `%listen`) chosen by the operator; the kernel does not enshrine a single source of truth.

2 Design Overview

There are three concrete kernel changes entailed by the Groundwire proposal:

1. **Jael-first comet keys.** Ames replaces `+request-attestation` with `+fetch-comet-pki`, which asks Jael for the comet's latest life and corresponding keys. If a record exists, Ames validates messages against it; otherwise, it may fall back to self-attestation. The authoritative store remains Jael's map from `$life` to `[crypto-suite=@ud =pass]` in `$point:jael`.
2. **Suite C tweaked keys.** We extend Suite B (`+crub`) to Suite C (`+cric`), which preserves Suite B and adds a case with tweaked signing keys. The untweaked signing public key and tweak data are included so any peer can reconstruct the tweaked key and verify it matches what the comet uses. In practice, current Groundwire comets commit to their ordinal; this prevents a wide class of replay and spoofing attacks and enables bidirectional provenance between on-chain and off-chain attestations.
3. **Fief-based routing.** We add an optional `$fief` field to comet entries in Jael defining a static IP/port or domain. Ames should attempt fief-based routing before sponsor-chain routing. It must not assume sponsor-chain termination at galaxies and must detect cycles.

The remainder of this article recaps elliptic-curve context and the current asymmetric cryptosuite interface used by Ames, then details the tweaked-key construction and routing implications. A prototype exists in Groundwire's forks of `urbit/urbit`, `urbit/vere`, and `urbit/urcrypt` implementing `+fetch-comet-pki`, `+cric`, and `$fief`.

3 Elliptic Curves

> Each Urbit ship possesses two networking keypairs: one for encryption, and one for authentication. We often refer to these two keypairs as though they were a single keypair because they are stored as a single atom. Elliptic Curve Diffie-Hellman is used for encryption, while Elliptic Curve Digital Signature Algorithm is used for authentication. (Urbit docs, "Ames Cryptography")

An *elliptic curve* is a two-dimensional curve defined by the general form $y^2 = x^3 + ax + b$ with the special condition that $4a^3 + 27b^2 \neq 0$. As long as that special condition holds true for whatever constants you picked for a and b, you can define a special type of addition for pairs of points on this curve where you draw a line between them, find the singular third point on the curve that this line hits, c, and then flip that third point across the x axis, $-c$ (see Figure 1). Multiplication means doing this process repeatedly.

What is the benefit of this? Its irreversibility. A private key is just a number; a public key is just that number multiplied by some other commonly agreed on number (the "base point") using elliptic curve arithmetic. Regular multiplication would mean that one could trivially obtain someone's private key by dividing their public key by the base point, but by bouncing all our operations around with elliptic curve multiplication, we prevent division. This is less crude and more beautiful than it might seem, because these keypairs have some special properties that are useful for cryptography.

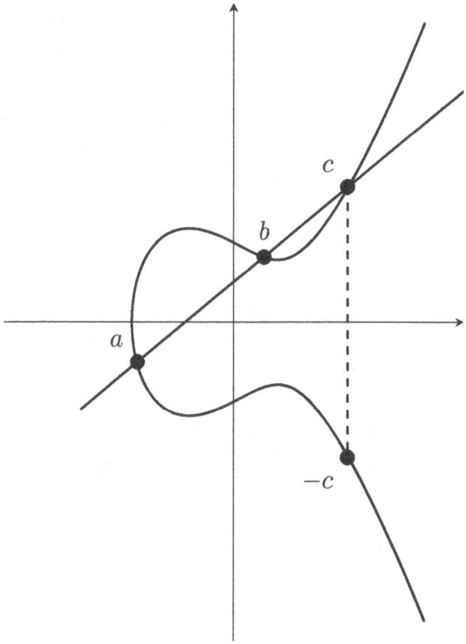

Figure 1: Elliptic curve point addition and multiplication, with the curve $y^2 = x^3 - x + 1$.

If Alice multiplies her private key by Bob's public key, Alice gets the same answer as if Bob multiplied his private key by Alice's public key. This allows the two parties to use that answer as a shared secret that only they know. In the *Elliptic Curve Diffie-Hellman* (ECDH) protocol, we take the x coordinate of that shared secret and run it through a key derivation function (in Urbit's case, SHA-256) to get a symmetric key which allows them to both encrypt and decrypt messages. Using this key, they can communicate privately.

Similarly, *Elliptic Curve Digital Signature Algorithm* (ECDSA) uses a more extensive algorithm to allow Alice to sign a message with her private key and for Bob to use his public key to verify that Alice did in fact sign it.

The elliptic curve that Urbit uses for key generation is the fast and un-patented *Curve25519*. This specifies the curve equation, the base point, and the finite field (the range of integers that we operate on, wrapping back to 0 if we go over the max value). There are two algebraically equivalent representations of Curve25519 that Urbit uses, with each defining its own set of standard operations: Montgomery Form (X25519), which is more efficient for ECDH, and Twisted Edwards Form (Ed25519), which is more efficient for EDDSA (an elliptic curve signature scheme similar to ECDSA).

Urbit implements the Ed25519 standard operations in its `+ed:crypto` zuse core for EDDSA, along with a few X25519-like operations for ECDH.

- `+scam`: scalar multiply. Takes a point and a scalar → returns scalar × point. This is the core elliptic curve operation.
- `+ward`: point addition (Edwards curve formula). Needed for scalar multiplication by repeated doubling-and-adding.
- `+etch`/`+deco`: encode/decode a curve point into/from an atom. This is how keys are serialized.
- `+luck`: derive a keypair (public plus private) from a seed. This is how comets/planets get Curve25519 keys.
- `+puck`: get the public key from a seed.
- `+slar`/`+shar`: perform a Diffie–Hellman secret derivation (ECDH). Given your private scalar and someone else's public point, return a shared secret.
- `+sign`/`+sign-raw`/`+sign-octs`: produce signatures. This is the ECDSA/EDDSA-like functionality.
- `+veri`/`+veri-octs`: verify signatures against a public key.

With all of this context, you can imagine why we'd want to have two pairs of networking keys: ECDH encryption and

EDDSA signatures are both complicated mathematical operations, so it's cleaner and safer to delineate between the two protocols completely in case of implementation bugs, future cryptographic discoveries, nonce reuse, and key rotations.

So how are these keypairs turned into an atom, where are they stored, and when are they used?

4 Asymmetric Cryptosuites

The usage of public and private keys we've described so far is called *asymmetric cryptography*. In current Arvo, the only existing implementation is `+crub:crypto` in zuse:

- `+seal`: encrypt to a peer. Runs ECDH with our encode secret plus their encode pubkey, hashes with SHA-256, signs with our auth secret, encrypts with AES-SIV.
- `+sign`: sign a message with our auth secret (EDDSA).
- `+sure`: verify a message was signed with the matching auth pubkey.
- `+tear`: decrypt from a peer. ECDH with our encrypt secret plus their encrypt pubkey, SHA-256, AES-SIV decrypt, then verify signature.
- `+fig`: SHA-256 fingerprint of the public key(s).
- `+pac`: SHA-256 fingerprint of the secret key(s).
- `+pub`: concatenate encode pubkey plus auth pubkey into one atom.
- `+sec`: concatenate encode secret plus auth secret into one atom.
- `+pit`: generate a new keypair from a seed. Uses SHA-512 for privates, `+puck:ed:crypto` for publics.
- `+nol`: reconstruct a `+crub` from a secret key atom.
- `+com`: reconstruct a `+crub` from a public key atom.

Here we have the key derivation and signing functions as wrappers around `+ed:crypto` and `+aes:crypto`, along with arms for turning networking keys into atoms and atoms back into ... `+crubs`? You'd think that we'd turn an atom back into a pair of networking keys. Right?

But what if you wanted to use a different cryptosuite with Ames? Then all of your old keys would be stranded as incompatible atoms. By using a `+crub` object instead, with keys in its payload and a battery for how to use them, we maintain consistency even if there were multiple implementations of `+acru`.

We do, then, need to track which cryptosuite to decode a key atom to—so we store this in the Jael secrets vane right next to the keys themselves:

```
+$  point
  $:  =rift
      =life
      keys=(map life [crypto-suite=@ud =pass])
      sponsor=(unit @p)
  ==
```

Now we can begin to home in on exactly what needs to change in the Urbit crypto suite in order for Groundwire to allow comets to rotate their keys.

In current Arvo (Listing 1), when a comet contacts another ship, that ship will ask the comet for an *unecrypted self-attestation packet* to prove that the sender does in fact control the private key whose public counterpart was hashed into the comet's `@p`.

But Groundwire comets don't self-attest to their identity; that attestation comes into Jael via `%ord-watcher` in the same way that Azimuth attestations come into Jael via `%azimuth` and `%eth-watcher`. In the Groundwire codebase, the `+request-attestation` arm is replaced with (Listing 2).

If we have this comet's networking keys in Jael (and thus `lyf` is not null), then instead of asking the comet to self-attest, we check our recorded networking keys. So far, so good: even though we're still expecting the comet's `@p` to match its public key in the non-Groundwire `?:` wutcol branch, we can skip that check and trust Jael for Groundwire comets. So why do we need to change our crypto suite?

5 Tweaked Keys

Groundwire's proposed change to comet attestation has greater philosophical implications for identity than you might expect.

Groundwire's strategy is to bet on Bitcoin being the one true long-term substrate that Urbit's PKI will live on, because Bitcoin is the only chain that offers an unambiguous protocol-level definition of canonical history ("the longest valid proof-of-work chain") that a zero-kelvin Urbit could resolve without appeal to social coordination or trusted checkpoints.

But it *is* a bet, and a contentious one at that in an ecosystem that includes Ethereum and Nockchain. For this reason, we *don't* insist that Jael only ingest comet PKI data from Bitcoin.

All of Groundwire's changes to Arvo stem from modifying Ames's `+request-attestation` arm to `+fetch-comet-pki`, with the core proposition being that comets have the ability to publish their networking keys to any source of PKI truth that other Urbit ships choose to interpret. To enable this, comets need to somehow encode within Jael *which* PKI they've attested to. This is where tweaked keys come in.

The payload of `+crub` is:

```
[pub=[cry=@ sgn=@] sek=(unit [cry=@ sgn=@])]
```

which are an encryption public key, a signing public key, and optionally their secret counterparts.

The Groundwire codebase introduces a new crypto-suite, `+cric`, with the payload:

```
$%  $:  suite=%b
        pub=[cry=@ sgn=@ ~]
        sek=$@(~ [sed=@ cry=@ sgn=@])
    ==
    $:  suite=%c
        pub=[cry=@ sgn=@ tw=[ugn=@ dat=@]]
        sek=$@(~ [sed=@ cry=@ sgn=@])
==  ==
```

Listing 1: The current Arvo comet handler.

```
::  +request-attestation: helper to request
::  attestation from comet. Also sets a timer
::  to resend the request every 30s.
::
++  request-attestation
  |=  =ship
  ^+  event-core
  =+  %^    ev-trace
          msg.veb
        ship
      |.("requesting attestion")
  =.  event-core
    =/  =blob  (sendkeys-packet ship)
    %:  send-blob
        for=|
        ship
        blob
        (~(get by peers.ames-state) ship)
    ==
  =/  =wire  /alien/(scot %p ship)
  (emit duct %pass wire %b %wait (add now ~s30))
```

Listing 2: The current Groundwire comet handler.

```
++  fetch-comet-pki
  |=  =ship
  ^+  event-core
  =+  %^    ev-trace
          msg.veb
        ship
      |.("requesting attestion")
  =/  lyf
    %:  rof
        [~ ~]
        /ames
        %j
        `beam`[[our %lyfe %da now] /(scot %p ship)]
    ==
  ?:  ?=([~ ~ [* * ^]] lyf)
    =.  event-core  (emil moves)
    %-  emit
      :*  [//keys]~
          %pass
          /public-keys
          %j
          %public-keys
          ship
          ~
          ~
      ==
  =.  event-core
    =/  =blob  (sendkeys-packet ship)
    %:  send-blob
        for=|
        ship
        blob
        (~(get by peers.ames-state) ship)
    ==
  =/  =wire  /alien/(scot %p ship)
  (emit duct %pass wire %b %wait (add now ~s30))
```

We refer to `+crub` as "Suite B" because it implements the NSA Suite B Cryptography Standard. `+cric` includes everything in Suite B, along with a new "Suite C" (a coinage of our own).

The Suite C payload's main difference is that the signing keys are "tweaked". We store `ugn`, the untweaked public key, and `sed`, the random seed used to originally generate our untweaked keypair, so that we have everything we need to recreate them if we ever need to. Then, we can tweak them by passing them into a tweaking function along with a bytestring, `dat` (omitting from our tweak the additional new field `xtr` which can include extra data):

```
::  pub.s = public signing key
::  sek.s = private signing key
=/  mit
  (shax (can 3 [32 pub.s] [(met 3 dat) dat] ~))
(scad:ed pub.s sek.s mit)
```

First, the public key is hashed along with the data to produce `mit`, the "tweak scalar." All three of these arguments get passed into `+scad:ed`, a wrapper around two other `+ed` arms:

```
::  scalar addition on public and private keys
++  scad
  ~/  %scad
  |=  [pub=@uxpoint sek=@uxscalar sca=@uxscalar]
  ^-  [pub=@uxpoint sek=@uxscalar]
  [(scap pub sca) (scas sek sca)]
```

These two arms, `+scap` and `+scas`, perform elliptic curve addition between the tweak scalar and corresponding key.

Anyone with both your public untweaked key and your tweak data can recreate your tweaked key. And, sure enough, we recall the `$point:jael` type:

```
+$  point
  $:  =rift
      =life
      keys=(map life [crypto-suite=@ud =pass])
      sponsor=(unit @p)
  ==
```

wherein the `pass` field is the atom that, in Suite B, encodes the two public keys. In Suite C, it encodes the encryption key, the untweaked signing key, *and* the tweak data. Upon receiving a message from a comet, your ship can reconstruct the tweaked key and check if it matches the key that the comet provides.

This might seem like a ton of unnecessary work. If you already trust Jael's sources of truth (`%ord-watcher`, in this case), why bother with tweaked keys at all?

The reason is that tweaking keys allows for a bidirectional cryptographic commitment between on-chain and off-chain attestations to prevent replay, spoofing, and double-spawning attacks. If there wasn't an off-chain anchor pointing to on-chain data, then anyone could come in and attest to ownership of any comet and `%ord-watcher` would naively believe them.

In Groundwire's implementation, that anchor is the ordinal number of the sat used for the comet's inscription. When `%ord-watcher` sees an attempted key rotation, it checks the specified comet identity's `$pass` in Jael to verify that the transaction's ordinal number matches the current tweak data, and rejects it if it doesn't. Back in userspace, any agent can later recompute the tweak to confirm that the key they're communicating with really does originate from the expected on-chain inscription.

This tweaked key protocol enables a new conception of identity on Urbit: rift, life, keys, *and data.*

6 Routing

The final implication of Groundwire's change to Ames' interpretation of comet provenance is that, since Groundwire comets articulate a network independent of Azimuth, they shouldn't need to rely on the current sponsorship hierarchy for packet routing. To facilitate this, comets can include include another piece of info in their attestations, called a `$fief`:

```
+$  fief
  $%  [%turf p=(list turf) q=@udE]
      [%if p=@ifF q=@udE]
      [%is p=@isH q=@udE]
  ==
```

in which `$point:jael` is updated to contain a `(unit fief)`, potentially storing the comet's static IP address (`%if` for IPv4 or `%is` for IPv6) or domain (`%turf`).

On top of this, Ames has been updated to allow any ship to be a valid sponsor, necessitating a few changes to its routing logic to detect cycles and ensure that sponsorship chains are allowed to terminate in any sponsor with a `$fief`, rather than only in galaxies.

Noun Serialization

Brian Klatt ~ticlys-monlun,
N. E. Davis ~lagrev-nocfep*
Zorp Corp

Abstract

Noun serialization is commonly used for Nock communication, both between instances like Urbit ships and with the runtime and the Unix host operating system. This article describes the principal convention for representing a noun in compressed form as a byte array and its runtime affordance.

Contents

*We gratefully acknowledge the original architect of `+jam` and `+cue`, Curtis Yarvin `~sorreg-namtyv`. The earliest implementation, in `jam.watt`, dates to ~2011.6.11; Yarvin has indicated that an earlier draft no longer survives.

Urbit Systems Technical Journal III:1 (2026): 83–101.
Address author correspondence to ~lagrev-nocfep.

1 Introduction

The Nock combinator calculus deals in nouns and does not know about bit encodings or memory layouts. A Nock interpreter (runtime) must, however, deal with the practicalities. In other words, there must be a way of writing down an abstract binary tree (consisting of cells/pairs and atoms) as an actual, physical array of bits in memory. Every possible Nock noun can be represented as a finite sequence of bytes (an atom), and there are multiple ways to do so.[1]

A noun serialization strategy is rather like a Gödel numbering in that it systematically encodes a mathematical object (a noun) as a number (an atom). Unlike Gödel numbering, which classically serially encodes the symbols of mathematical statements, noun serialization encodes a binary tree structure.[2] Because a noun may be any atom—and atoms cannot have leading zeroes—both structure and value need to be unambiguously encoded and cannot be simply delimited (as by a `0` bit or similar). Run-length serialization, with or without references, forms the basis of practical strategies to encode a noun as an atom. This embodies a tradeoff between simplicity, size, and speed. We describe this strategy and some pedagogical variants which afford insight to the process. Likewise, deserialization is the inverse operation of converting a serialized atom back into the original noun, and must be unambiguously reversible. Noun serialization is essential for Nock communication, both between Nock execution layers such as Vere and NockVM, and between the runtime and the host operating system.

2 Naïve Serialization

A noun may be an atom or a cell, and so we first propose to label nodes by type, with `0` for atom and `1` for cell.

---

[1]The converse is not true: not every atom represents a valid deserialization or conversion from a graph encoding.

[2]This also echoes the way that S-expressions are encoded in Lisp.

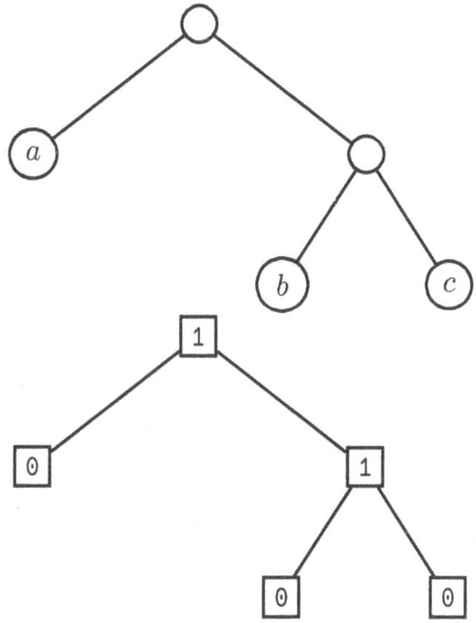

Figure 1: The noun `[a b c]` (the same as `[a [b c]]`) as a binary tree and its metadata labeling in the simplest scheme.

The noun in Figure 1 is represented as a binary tree, where each node is labeled with its type (atom or cell) and its value (if applicable). To serialize this noun, we can perform a pre-order traversal of the tree, recording the type and value of each node. The serialized form would be (in LSB order):

```
c 0 b 0 1 a 0 1
```

The issue, however, is that in decoding this bitstream we do not know where an atom value (such as `a`) ends. After all, the point of serialization is to be able to deserialize the bitstream back into the original noun. Thus we need a way to indicate the length of each atom.

2.1 Atom Length Encoding

Let's augment this scheme by providing length information for each atom. One basic idea is to include a string of `0` bits as the least-significant bits (LSB) of the atom which indicates the length of the atom in bits. Since the atom could be zero, we also delimit the length with a `1` bit. (See Table 1 for examples.)

$$a = a_{\ell-1}a_{\ell-2}\ldots a_1 a_0 \xrightarrow[\text{encode}]{} \bar{a} = a_{\ell-1}a_{\ell-2}\ldots a_1 a_0\ \mathtt{1}\ \mathtt{0}^n,$$

where $\bar{a}$ is the encoded atom a and a has length ℓ bits.[3] This is a unary run-length encoding (RLE) using zeros.[4]

Table 1: Example atom encodings with length information appended as trailing zeros (unnamed encoding). Elided digits are shown in light gray for clarity.

Atom a	**Length (bits)**	**Encoded Form $\bar{a}$**
`0b0`	1	`0b01`
`0b1`	1	`0b110`
`0b10`	2	`0b10100`
`0b11`	2	`0b11100`
`0b101`	3	`0b1011000`
`0b111`	3	`0b1111000`
`0x70`	7	`0b11100001000000`
`0xff`	8	`0b1111111110000000`
`0x1234`	13	`0b100100011010010000000000000`

We can make one further optimization: since the most significant bit (MSB) of the atom is always `1` except in the case of zero (which is `0b1` with the leading zero trimmed), we can omit it from the encoded form. This saves one bit for every non-zero atom. Let's call this scheme `+fat` encoding. (See Table 2 for examples.)

`+fat` Serialization Algorithm

- **Encode**. Write[5] ℓ bits of `0`, where ℓ is the length of a in

[3]We will use the overbar notation $\bar{a}$ throughout to notionally indicate the encoded form of a, regardless of the method used.

[4]Zero is something of a "special case": it has no length and leading zeros are trimmed, so its encoding consists only of the delimiter, `0b1`.

[5]We always say this from the LSB, so from the right as written on the page.

unary, followed by `1`. The next ℓ bits are the atom a in binary without the leading `1`.

- **Decode**. Read the unary length ℓ by counting `0` bits until the first `1` bit. Read the next ℓ bits to get the atom a without the leading `1`. Prepend a `1` bit to a unless ℓ is zero, in which case the atom is zero.

Table 2: Example atom encodings (`+fat` encoding). Elided digits are shown in light gray for clarity.

Atom a	Length (bits)	Encoded Form $\bar{a}$
`0b0`	1	`0b1`
`0b1`	1	`0b 10`
`0b10`	2	`0b 100`
`0b11`	2	`0b 1100`
`0b101`	3	`0b 11000`
`0b111`	3	`0b 111000`
`0x70`	7	`0b 11000010000000`
`0xff`	8	`0b 1111111100000000`
`0x1234`	13	`0b 1000110100100000000000000`

The primary problem with the `+fat` scheme is that the encoding of an atom is about twice the bit length of the original atom. The next optimization is to use the bit length of the unary bit length, which is logarithmic in the bit length.

$$a = \underbrace{a_{\ell-1}a_{\ell-2}\ldots a_1 a_0}_{\ell = \underbrace{\ell_{h-1}\ell_{h-2}\ldots\ell_1\ell_0}_{h}}$$

$$\begin{aligned} a &= a_{\ell-1}a_{\ell-2}\ldots a_1 a_0 \xrightarrow[\texttt{+mat}\text{ encode}]{} \\ \bar{a} &= \underbrace{a_{\ell-1}a_{\ell-2}\ldots a_1 a_0}_{\ell}\underbrace{\ell_{h-2}\ell_{h-1}\ldots\ell_1\ell_0}_{h-1}1\underbrace{\texttt{0}\ldots\texttt{0}}_{h}, \end{aligned}$$

where ℓ is the bit length of a and h is the "hyper bit length" of a. This yields a bit length encoding of $1 + 2\log_2(\ell)$ bits rather than 2ℓ bits. This scheme is called `+mat` encoding, and it is currently in use as an internal auxiliary format for other serializations.

`+mat` Serialization Algorithm

- **Encode**. Write the number h of `0` bits in unary, followed a leading `1` and then $h-1$ bits for the low bits of ℓ. The next ℓ bits are the atom a in binary.
- **Decode**. Read the unary length of the length h by counting `0` bits (from the LSB/right) until the first `1` bit. Read the next $h-1$ bits to get $\ell-1$, the bit length of the atom. Finally, read the next ℓ bits (adding the leading `1`) to get the atom a.

Some worked examples of `+mat` encoding are included in Table 3.

The reference implementation of `+mat` encoding in Hoon is as follows:

```
++  mat
  ~/  %mat
  |=  a=@
  ^-  [p=@ q=@]
  ?:  =(0 a)
    [1 1]
  =+  b=(met 0 a)
  =+  c=(met 0 b)
  :-  (add (add c c) b)
  (cat 0 (bex c) (mix (end [0 (dec c)] b)
   ↳                    (lsh [0 (dec c)] a)))
```

Table 3: Example atom encodings (`+mat` encoding). The encoded form is the same result as `q:(mat a)` in Hoon.

Atom a	**Length (bits)**	**Mathematics**	**Encoded Form** $\bar{a}$
`0b0`	$\ell = 1$	$\underbrace{\cancel{a_{\ell-1}\cdots a_0}}_{\ell=0}\ \ 1\underbrace{\cancel{0\ldots0}}_{h=0}$	`0b1`
`0b1`	$\ell = 1$	$\underbrace{1}_{\ell=1}\underbrace{\cancel{\ell_{h-2}\cdots\ell_0}}_{h-1=0}\ \ 1\underbrace{0}_{h=1}$	`0b110`
`0b10`	$\ell = 2$	$\underbrace{10}_{a=2}\ \underbrace{0}_{\text{low bits of }\ell}\ \ 1\underbrace{00}_{h=2}$	`0b100100`
`0b11`	$\ell = 2$	$\underbrace{11}_{a=3}\ \underbrace{0}_{\text{low bits of }\ell}\ \ 1\underbrace{00}_{h=2}$	`0b110100`
`0b100`	$\ell = 3$	$\underbrace{100}_{a=4}\ \underbrace{1}_{\text{low bits of }\ell}\ \ 1\underbrace{00}_{h=2}$	`0b1001100`
`0b101`	$\ell = 3$	$\underbrace{101}_{a=5}\ \underbrace{1}_{\text{low bits of }\ell}\ \ 1\underbrace{00}_{h=2}$	`0b1011100`
`0b1111`	$\ell = 4$	$\underbrace{1111}_{a=15}\ \underbrace{00}_{\text{low bits of }\ell}\ \ 1\underbrace{000}_{h=3}$	`0b1111001000`
`0x70`	$\ell = 7$	$\underbrace{1110000}_{a=112}\ \underbrace{11}_{\text{low bits of }\ell}\ \ 1\underbrace{000}_{h=3}$	`0b1110000111000`
`0x1234`	$\ell = 13$	$\underbrace{1001000110100}_{a=4660}\ \underbrace{101}_{\text{low bits of }\ell}\ \ 1\underbrace{0000}_{h=4}$	`0b1001000110100101110000`

With `+mat` encoding in hand, we can produce a proper serialization scheme for nouns by combining the type bit with the encoded atom or recursively encoding cells. We call this scheme `+gel` encoding.

As before, we use `0` for atom and `1` for cell. If the noun is an atom, we follow the type bit with the `+mat` encoding of the atom. If the noun is a cell, we follow the type bit with the `+gel` encoding of the head and then the `+gel` encoding of the tail.

Consider the noun `[4 [0 1]]` (= `[4 0 1]`), represented as a binary tree in Figure 2. Reading across in a depth-first traversal, we produce an encoding order:

```
(mat 1)(0)(mat 0)(0)(1)(mat 4)(0)(1)
```

We already have the `+mat` encodings from Table 3; substituting these in yields:

```
[110](0)[1](0)(1)[1001100](0)(1)
0b110.0.1.0.1.1001100.0.1
0b1100101100110001
```

`+gel` Serialization Algorithm

- **Encode**.
  - If the noun is an atom, write `0` followed by the `+mat` encoding of the atom.
  - If the noun is a cell, write `1` followed by the `+gel` encoding of the head and then the `+gel` encoding of the tail.
- **Decode**. Read the first bit.
  - If it is `0`, read the next bits as a `+mat` encoded atom.
  - If it is `1`, recursively read the next bits as the head and then the tail.

`+gel` encoding is straightforward to read and write even by hand. Worked examples are included in Table 4.

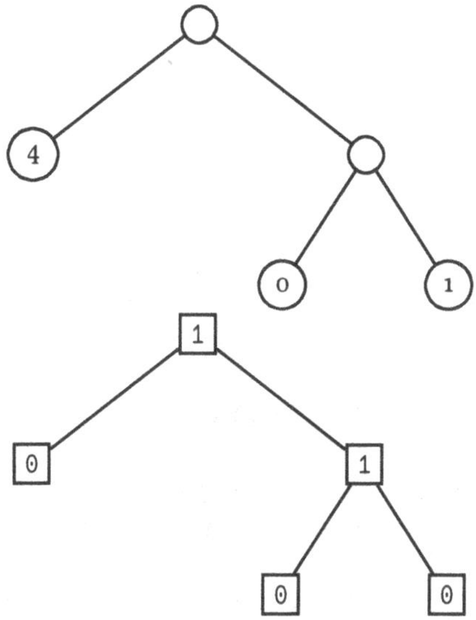

Figure 2: The noun `[4 0 1]` as a binary tree and its metadata labeling in the simplest scheme. Compare Figure 1.

Our code implementation for `+gel` encoding is as follows:

```
++  gel
  |=  a=*
  ^-  @
  =+  b=0
  =<  q
  |-  ^-  [p=@ q=@]
  ?:  ?=(@ a)
    =+  d=(mat a)
    [(add 1 p.d) (lsh 0 q.d)]
  =>  .(b (add 1 b))
  =+  d=$(a -.a)
  =+  e=$(a +.a, b (add b p.d))
  :-  (add 1 (add p.d p.e))
  (mix 1 (lsh [0 1] (cat 0 q.d q.e)))
```

Decoding is left as an exercise to the motivated reader.

Table 4: Example noun encodings (`+gel` encoding). `.` dot delimits bit fields for readability.

Noun	Encoded Form
`0`	`0b0.1.0`
`[0 0]`	`0b1.0.1.0.1`
`[1 0]`	`0b1.0.110.0.1`
`[2 1 0]`	`0b1.0.110.0.1.100100.0.1`
`[[2 3] 1 0]`	`0b1.0.110.0.1.110100.0.100100.0.1.1`

3 Practical Serialization

Whatever the pedagogical advantages of `+gel`, the algorithm is still relatively verbose. Nock-based operating functions have preferred in practice to use `+jam` encoding, which is a more compact run-length encoding with subtree deduplication.[6] `+jam` improves the basic strategy by altering the RLE algorithm slightly and supporting internal references for noun subtrees that have already been encoded.

`+jam` converts a noun into a buffer and deduplicates repeated subtrees. It walks subtrees and encodes each in a way that allows for efficient storage and retrieval, while also permitting references to previously encoded values. Basically, it takes `+gel` and adds a "caching mode" flag; instead of repeating subtrees, encode the index in the full jammed noun to where the current node's jammed subnoun was first written. Thus the code changes from `0` for atom and `1` for cell to:

- `0` for atom.
- `01` for cell.
- `11` for cached node.

Following the metadata labels given in Figure 3, the encoding order for `[[0 0] 0 0]` is:

[6]Note the calculation of `~dozreg-toplud`, p. 57 of this issue, that an operational Arvo instance may have up to 1.66×10^{21} nouns, greatly reduced by structural sharing.

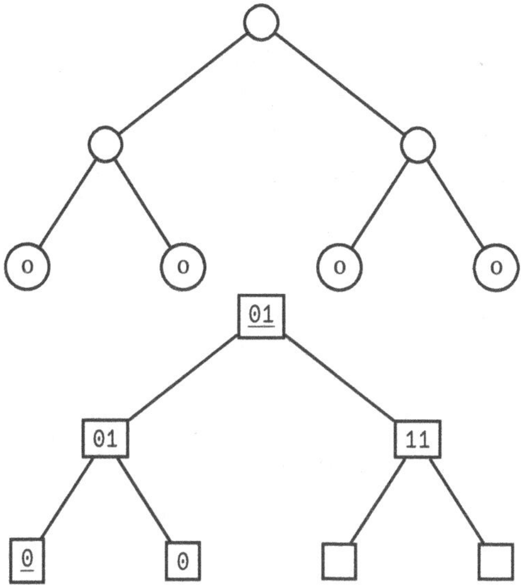

Figure 3: The noun `[[0 0] 0 0]` as a binary tree and its metadata labeling for the `+jam` scheme.

```
(mat 2)(11)(mat 0)(0)(mat 0)(0)(01)(01)
0b100100.11.1.0.1.0.01.01
0b1001001110100101
```

The cached entry `(mat 2)` indicates that the cached subtree is a copy of the subtree located at tree address 2 in the overall jammed noun.

However, this bit of cleverness isn't the end: `+jam` also decides *when* to cache subtrees based on the size of the nouns involved. For instance, `[3 3 3]` encodes as:

```
(mat 3)(0)(mat 3)(0)(01)(mat 3)(0)(01)
0b110100.0.110100.0.01.110100.0.01
0b11010001101000011101000001
```

wherein no caching is used. When 3 is first encountered at index 2, 2 and 3 have the same bit lengths; since `(mat 2)` and `(mat 3)` are the same length, caching would not save any space and would add decoding overhead due to dereferencing.

In contrast, `[4 4 4]` encodes as:

```
(mat 2)(11)(mat 2)(11)(01)(1001100)(0)(01)
0b100100.11.100100.11.01.1001100.0.01
0b10010011100100110110011000001
```

where caching is used for the second and third occurrences of 4. Here, 4 has bit length 3 which is greater than the bit length of 2 which is 2, and caching saves space overall in the jammed noun.

`+jam` Serialization Algorithm

- **Encode**.
  - If the noun is an atom, write `0` followed by the `+mat` encoding of the atom.
  - If the noun is a cell, check if it has been previously encoded.
    - If it has, write `11` followed by the `+mat` encoding of the index where it was first encoded.
    - If it has not, write `01` followed by the `+jam` encoding of the head and then the `+jam` encoding of the tail. Store the current index for future reference.
- **Decode**. Read the first bit.
  - If it is `0`, read the next bits as a `+mat` encoded atom.
  - If it is `1`, read the next bit.
    - If it is `0`, recursively read the next bits as the head and then the tail.
    - If it is `1`, read the next bits as a `+mat` encoded index and retrieve the cached subtree.

Here is the reference implementation of `+jam` in Hoon:

```
++  jam
  ~/  %jam
  |=  a=*
  ^-  @
  =+  b=0
```

```
  =+  m=`(map * @)`~
  =<  q
  |-  ^-  [p=@ q=@ r=(map * @)]
  =+  c=(~(get by m) a)
  ?~  c
    =>  .(m (~(put by m) a b))
    ?:  ?=(@ a)
      =+  d=(mat a)
      [(add 1 p.d) (lsh 0 q.d) m]
    =>  .(b (add 2 b))
    =+  d=$(a -.a)
    =+  e=$(a +.a, b (add b p.d), m r.d)
    :+  (add 2 (add p.d p.e))
      (mix 1 (lsh [0 2] (cat 0 q.d q.e)))
    r.e
  ?:  ?&(?=(@ a) (lte (met 0 a) (met 0 u.c)))
    =+  d=(mat a)
    [(add 1 p.d) (lsh 0 q.d) m]
  =+  d=(mat u.c)
  [(add 2 p.d) (mix 3 (lsh [0 2] q.d)) m]
```

A Python implementation of `+jam` is included in the appendix.

Here is the reference implementation of `+cue` in Hoon:

```
++  cue
  ~/  %cue
  |=  a=@
  ^-  *
  =+  b=0
  =+  m=`(map @ *)`~
  =<  q
  |-  ^-  [p=@ q=* r=(map @ *)]
  ?:  =(0 (cut 0 [b 1] a))
    =+  c=(rub +(b) a)
    [+(p.c) q.c (~(put by m) b q.c)]
  =+  c=(add 2 b)
  ?:  =(0 (cut 0 [+(b) 1] a))
    =+  u=$(b c)
    =+  v=$(b (add p.u c), m r.u)
    =+  w=[q.u q.v]
    [(add 2 (add p.u p.v)) w (~(put by r.v) b w)]
  =+  d=(rub c a)
```

```
  [(add 2 p.d) (need (~(get by m) q.d)) m]
::  length decode
++  rub
  ~/  %rub
  |=  [a=@ b=@]
  ^-  [p=@ q=@]
  =+  ^=  c
      =+  [c=0 m=(met 0 b)]
      |-  ?<  (gth c m)
      ?.  =(0 (cut 0 [(add a c) 1] b))
        c
      $(c +(c))
  ?:  =(0 c)
    [1 0]
  =+  d=(add a +(c))
  =+  e=(add (bex (dec c)) (cut 0 [d (dec c)] b))
  [(add (add c c) e) (cut 0 [(add d (dec c)) e] b)]
```

Likewise, a Python implementation of `+cue` is included in the appendix.

3.1 `newt` Encoding

"Newt" encoding is a runtime-oriented extension of `+jam`based noun serialization which adds a short identifying header in case of future changes to the runtime's serialization format. A version number (currently a single bit) precedes a RLE serialization length followed by the `+jam` serialization of the noun. The version number is currently `0b0`.

```
V.LLLL.JJJJ.JJJJ.JJJJ.JJJJ.JJJJ.JJJJ
```

where `V` is the version number, `L` is the total length of the noun in bytes, and `J` is the `+jam` serialization of the noun.

Runtime communications vanes like `%khan` and `%lick` utilize this encoding locally. It is exclusively used as a host OS runtime affordance at the current time.

4 Conclusion

Noun serialization is a fundamental aspect of Urbit's architecture, enabling efficient communication of untyped data structures. Starting from basic run-length encoding, we have explored progressively more sophisticated schemes culminating in `+jam`, which balances compactness and efficiency through subtree deduplication. Further extensions like `newt` illustrate the adaptability of serialization strategies to meet evolving runtime requirements. As Nock-based solid-state computing continues to evolve, noun serialization will remain an important foundation for data interchange and persistence.

Appendix: Python +jam/+cue

Paul Driver ~fodwyt-ragful

The following is a simple Python implementation of +jam serialization and +cue deserialization drawn from Urbit's auxiliary pynoun library.

```
from bitstring import BitArray
noun = int | Cell
# The Cell class represents an ordered pair of two nouns.
def jam_to_stream(n: noun, out: BitArray):
    """jam but put the bits into a stream
    >>> s = BitArray()
    >>> jam_to_stream(Cell(0,0), s)
    >>> s
    BitArray('0b100101')
    """

    cur = 0
    refs = {}

    def bit(b: bool):
        nonlocal cur
        out.append([b])
        cur += 1

    def zero():
        bit(False)

    def one():
        bit(True)

    def bits(num: int, count: int):
        nonlocal cur
        for i in range(0, count):
            out.append([(num & (1 << i)) != 0])
        cur += count

    def save(a: noun):
        refs[a] = cur
```

```
def mat(i: int):
    if 0 == i:
        one()
    else:
        a = i.bit_length()
        b = a.bit_length()
        above = b + 1
        below = b - 1
        bits(1 << b, above)
        bits(a & ((1 << below) - 1), below)
        bits(i, a)

def back(ref: int):
    one()
    one()
    mat(ref)

def r(a: noun):
    dupe = refs.get(a)
    if deep(a):
        if dupe:
            back(dupe)
        else:
            save(a)
            one()
            zero()
            r(a.head)
            r(a.tail)
    elif dupe:
        isize = a.bit_length()
        dsize = dupe.bit_length()
        if isize < dsize:
            zero()
            mat(a)
        else:
            back(dupe)
    else:
        save(a)
        zero()
        mat(a)
r(n)
```

```
def jam(n: noun):
    """urbit serialization: * -> @

    >>> jam(0)
    2
    >>> jam(Cell(0,0))
    41
    >>> jam(Cell(Cell(1234567890987654321, \\
    ...                1234567890987654321), \\
    ...           Cell(1234567890987654321, \\
    ...                1234567890987654321)))
    22840095095806892874257389573
    """

    out = BitArray()
    jam_to_stream(n, out)
    return read_int(len(out), out)

def cue_from_stream(s: BitArray):
    """cue but read the bits from a stream
    >>> s = BitArray('0b01')
    >>> cue_from_stream(s)
    0
    """

    refs = {}
    cur = 0
    position = 0

    def bits(n: int):
        nonlocal cur, position
        cur += n
        result = 0
        for i in range(n):
            result |= (1 if s[position] else 0) << i
            position += 1
        return result

    def one():
        nonlocal cur, position
        cur += 1
        bit = s[position]
```

```
            position += 1
            return bit

    def rub():
        z = 0
        while not one():
            z += 1
        if 0 == z:
            return 0
        below = z - 1
        lbits = bits(below)
        bex = 1 << below
        return bits(bex ^ lbits)

    def r(start: int):
        ret = None
        if one():
            if one():
                ret = refs[rub()]
            else:
                hed = r(cur)
                tal = r(cur)
                ret = Cell(hed, tal)
        else:
            ret = rub()
        refs[start] = ret
        return ret
    return r(cur)

def cue(i: int):
    """urbit deserialization: @ -> *

    >>> str(cue(22840095095806892874257389573))
    '[[1234567890987654321 1234567890987654321]
      1234567890987654321 1234567890987654321]'
    """

    bits = BitArray()
    while i > 0:
        bits.append([i & 1 == 1])
        i >>= 1
    return cue_from_stream(bits)
```

Obelisk is a novel relational database management system (RDBMS) and its scripting language, urQL, designed for the experimental Urbit computing platform but adaptable to other systems.

Building on E. F. Codd's relational algebra and unencumbered by backward compatibility constraints, Obelisk is a temporal relational database derived from first principles. Key innovations include time travel for querying historical database states, proper set implementation, elimination of nulls, idempotent queries, and enforced com-posability. Obelisk ensures all user operations are accessible via both the urQL scripting language and API, reflecting Urbit's pure functional architecture.

Obelisk's time-travel f[illegible]ture indexes every schema and content [illegible] change by time, ensuring idempotent queries and atomic scri[illegible] execution. This paper explor[illegible]ces relational database design while addressing SQL's [illegible]ficiencies, offering a mod[illegible] structured data management.

Obelisk: Reinventing SQL for Modern Computing

Jack Fox ~nomryg-nilref
FoxyLabs

Abstract

Obelisk is a novel relational database management system and its scripting language, urQL, designed for the experimental Urbit computing platform but adaptable to other systems. Building on E. F. Codd's relational algebra and unencumbered by backward compatibility constraints, Obelisk is a temporal relational database derived from first principles. Key innovations include time travel for querying historical database states, proper set implementation, elimination of nulls, idempotent queries, and enforced composability. Obelisk ensures all user operations are accessible via both the urQL scripting language and API, reflecting Urbit's pure functional architecture. Obelisk's time-travel feature indexes every schema and content state change by time, ensuring idempotent queries and atomic script execution. This paper explores how Obelisk advances relational database design while addressing SQL's deficiencies, offering a modern, principled approach to structured data management.

Contents

Urbit Systems Technical Journal III:1 (2026): 103–132.
Address author correspondence to ~nomryg-nilref.

1 Introduction

The Obelisk relational database management system (RDBMS) and urQL scripting language[1] run on the experimental Urbit computer and network but could just as well be implemented on any other computer—except for certain features dependent on Hoon language features or the Urbit network architecture.[2]

---

[1]We prefer *scripting language* over *query language* for semantic reasons. It does more than query.

[2]Notably subnet security features and shrubbery enabling `SELECT` statements.

Like all relational databases, it is built upon E. F. Codd's pioneering computer science work developing the relational algebra and uniting it with set theory and predicate calculus.[3] As relational databases implementing SQL came to dominate structured data storage the SQL standard evolved, always bearing, and hindered by, the necessary constraint of backward compatibility. As the first and only RDBMS for a new computing paradigm, Obelisk has no obligation to the past and so is free to build anew from first principles with all the learnings of the last half century while perpetuating the best features of SQL.

Obelisk's urQL, while clearly a dialect of SQL, fixes numerous deficiencies in SQL[4], elevates composability to a syntactic requirement (not merely an option), adds one completely new major feature, time travel,[5] and leaves no functionality inaccessible to the normal user.

The RDBMS evolution that is Obelisk was greatly inspired by the Urbit architecture. Urbit is a computer whose entire state (OS and userspace) is a pure function of its prior state.[6] The Urbit computer itself is an ACID database. The entire state of the server is one noun[7] that advances only through pure functions. urQL's syntax is more than a "better" scripting language, it is an accurate reflection of the underlying database server's operations. Anything the user can accomplish through urQL they

[3] Codd (1970); Chamberlin and Boyce (1974) Codd's seminal paper focuses primarily on studying set relations and does not invent a query language, but sets out the parameters for an effective and efficient language. Predicate calculus was already the obvious way to filter stored data. Chamberlin and Boyce (1974) treat it as a given, discussing their syntax for applying it.

[4] E.g. the SQL standard does not truly implement sets by default. Obelisk does.

[5] Darwen and Date (1998); Darwen and Date (2002). While influential in other aspects of Obelisk's design. We are less familiar with their work on temporal databases, so their research on temporal databases was not especially influential. Without any direct knowledge of his work, we credit the reputation of Rich Hickey.

[6] ~sorreg-namtyv et al. (2016). Is any sufficiently complex computer function completely pure? Urbit and Obelisk both rely on crash to reject invalid commands that parsing and the API type system cannot otherwise validate.

[7] The *noun* is an Urbit abstraction that maps beautifully to English. It is either a natural number, or an ordered pair of nouns. Thus the fundamental data structure of Urbit (and Obelisk) is a binary tree of natural numbers.

can also do through the API[8], and vice versa. Together with Obelisk's native time travel capabilities and idempotence, there are no mysteries confronting the user, no functionality outside the scope of the API/scripting language like performing audits with database logs. There are no logs. (There are system views that emulate logs to support the familiar log analysis pattern.) Obelisk's state is both its current state and all prior states.[9]

Obelisk's major innovations include:

- Time travel
- Proper sets
- No nulls
- Composability

2 Time Travel

> The totality of data in a data bank may be viewed as a collection of time-varying relations (Codd, 1970).

In Obelisk time is primary and fundamental. Every change of state, whether to a database's schema or content, is indexed by time. Thus every query is idempotent because each query is implicitly or explicitly associated with a particular state in the series. And time is a series of steps, like in physical reality. A time step may be appended to the series, but there is no inserting, updating, or deleting time steps.

The rules enforcing time primacy in the Obelisk database engine are simple. Each database holds a most recent schema[10] time (by user data table) and a most recent content time (by user data table). Every subsequent state change, whether to schema or content must be subsequent to the latest of the two

[8]Of the SQL RDBMSs that do have APIs, they are uniformly bolted-on afterthoughts.

[9]With the sole exception of dropping a database from the server, in which case all traces of the database vanish from the server.

[10]Currently the only schema altering commands available are `CREATE` and `DROP`. `ALTER` is on the roadmap for an undetermined future release.

times. Normally the user never needs to concern themselves with this requirement. When not overridden by `AS OF` the database engine applies the host ship's time[11] to determine the current state of the database.

Script execution, regardless of the number or sequencing of commands, potentially alters the state of the database as if everything happened *all at once*, even though the commands execute sequentially. Users only need to be aware of this rule when applying `AS OF` to override `NOW`. It is possible for a script to result in different ending state times for different tables. Violation of time constraints (or any other error) causes the entire script to fail. (Scripts are always atomic.)

The second and final rule is once a script introduces a query—a `SELECT` command returning data results (but not any intermediate `SELECT`)—all subsequent commands must also be queries. Further schema or data changes are not allowed.

Among the metadata returned by queries are the schema and content times (labelled `schema time` and `data time`) used by the engine to create the query results. A query executes with a *de facto* time of the latest of the two for the state of each underlying table or view. In order to recreate the same query one needs to specify this `AS OF` time. Thus every query is implicitly or explicitly idempotent.

Creating a new schema component, `DATABASE`, `NAMESPACE`,[12] `TABLE`, or `VIEW`, may be backdated (or forward dated) to any time subsequent to the latest of schema time or content time (`CREATE DATABASE` is of course entirely independent). Users override schema and data manipulation commands at their own peril. It is possible to effectively lock all or portions of the database for update.

```
CREATE DATABASE db2 AS OF ~2099.1.1 ;

%obelisk-result:
```

[11] A *ship* is the generic term for an Urbit computer on the Urbit network, which has a unique, immutable, cryptographically protected identity. The ship's time corresponds to the computer time on the Urbit VM's host computer, whether Linux/Unix, Mac, or Windows.

[12] A *namespace* is known as *schema* in the rest of the SQL world, leading to confusion.

```
  %results
    [ %message 'created database %db2' ]
    [ %server-time ~2024.9.29..21.14.00..7fc8 ]
    [ %schema-time ~2099.1.1 ]
```

Getting passing results for all operations on the database now requires a time subsequent to this future creation date.

```
(crash)
CREATE NAMESPACE: %ns1 as-of schema time out of order
```

The database is not even visible in the current context.

```
FROM sys.sys.databases AS OF NOW
SELECT * ;
```

```
%obelisk-result:
  %results
    [ %message 'SELECT' ]
    %result-set
      database  sys-agent  sys-tmsp  data-ship
       ↳ data-agent  data-tmsp
      db1  /gall/dojo  ~2024.9.26
       ↳ ~zod  /gall/dojo  ~2024.9.26
      sys  /gall/dojo  ~2024.9.26
       ↳ ~zod  /gall/dojo  ~2024.9.26
    [ %server-time ~2024.9.26..22.03.39..2233 ]
    [ %message 'sys.sys.databases' ]
    [ %schema-time ~2024.9.26 ]
    [ %data-time ~2024.9.26 ]
    [ %vector-count 2 ]
```

We can see it in a future time context.

```
FROM sys.sys.databases AS OF ~2099.1.1
SELECT * ;
```

```
database  sys-agent  sys-tmsp  data-ship
 ↳ data-agent  data-tmsp
animal-shelter  /gall/dojo  ~2024.10.1
 ↳ ~zod  /gall/dojo  ~2024.10.1
db1  /gall/dojo  ~2024.9.26
 ↳ ~zod  /gall/dojo  ~2024.9.26
db2  /gall/dojo  ~2099.1.1
 ↳ ~zod  /gall/dojo  ~2030.1.1
```

```
sys  /gall/dojo  ~2024.9.26
 ↳ ~zod  /gall/dojo  ~2024.9.26
```

Manipulating AS OF time for schema components is rarely useful, but could be used for creating and populating a database with history. What is much more useful is setting the content time for query or content manipulation[13] relative to some past state, or mixing times to audit content changes.

```
FROM my-table T1
OUTER JOIN my-table AS OF <some past date> T2
WHERE NOT EXISTS T1.key
   OR NOT EXISTS T2.key
SELECT * ;
```

(The example demonstrates urQL's non-standard join and predicate syntax. A full explanation of these follows.)

The astute reader may have already inferred the missing piece of the time travel puzzle. When specified in a FROM clause, the database engine will use the closest content state less than or equal to the time requested, using the table schema in a state likewise less than or equal to that time.

Suppose that my-table has content mutated at two times, ~2024.10.2..16.54.41..df15 and ~2024.10.4..17.32.11..a1c2.

```
FROM db2..my-table-1 AS OF ~2024.10.3
SELECT * ;


%obelisk-result:
  %results
    [ %message 'SELECT' ]
    %result-set

      <results not shown>

    [ %server-time ~2024.10.30..17.00.48..85c2 ]
    [ %message 'db1.dbo.my-table-1' ]
    [ %schema-time ~2023.1.4..14.15.21..ad17 ]
    [ %data-time ~2024.10.2..16.54.41..df15 ]
    [ %vector-count 3 ]
```

[13]Setting the AS OF time when manipulating data (INSERT, UPDATE, DELETE) results in a new content state based on the state in effect at that time.

As explained above, the database engine returns metadata for this query which allows us to identify the implicit idempotent query. Any `AS OF` time `>=` `~2024.10.2..16.54.41..df15` and `<` `~2024.10.4..17.32.11..a1c2` is the same idempotent query.

```
FROM db2..my-table-1 AS OF ~2024.10.2..16.54.41..df15
SELECT * ;
```

Identifying *the* idempotent query with the one exactly matching the content state time is important. The current last content state in the table's series can always be superseded by a content state one tick later.

Idempotent queries have a big technical benefit. The engine can cache query results with never a thought given to cache expiration. Simple systems have fewer bugs and less attack surface. Obelisk does this for views—which in Obelisk are read only. Making a long-running query a view requires only a one-time performance hit...until the backing table data state progresses, in which case there is another one-time performance hit.

3 The Relational Model

3.1 Relations

So far we have casually referred to *tables* and *views* as standard components of relational databases. In this section we introduce Codd's term, *relation*.[14] (What follows is a hasty summary of Codd's formal definition, and it is somewhat more restrictive than Codd's definition in order to make a further point below.) Consider a proper set of data tuples (i.e. every member unique). All the tuples have the same length, and positionally each element across the tuples is of the same type. This is a relation. Arranging the tuples as rows in a 2D matrix (arbitrarily ordered), we can index the columns by unique labels.[15]

[14] Codd (1970).

[15] Here we deviate from Codd's formal definition, where he only suggests the columns—he has formally defined them as domains—may be labeled, the

We can refer to each element in the tuples by the column label, yielding a definition of relation for the discussion below.

3.2 Proper sets

There is no `DISTINCT` keyword. All relations in Obelisk are proper sets, as Codd intended.

A *table* in Obelisk is a set of immutable persistently stored relations—indexed by time. Rows are indexed by a unique key referencing one or more column names, which ensures a proper set. Mutating the contents results in a new subsequent relation.

A *view* is a persistently *defined* relation. It is defined by `SELECT` commands and set operators over tables and views. The relation's set-like characteristic is maintained by shrinking the rows to a proper set. Views are indexed by time. A change to the definition or state of any table referenced in the definition results in a new time index. As mentioned earlier, if a user queries a view the system caches its state for that point in time. We distinguish between *persistently defined* and *persistently stored* because there is no requirement for view data to persist. Due to query idempotence it can always be recreated.

The `SELECT` command is a special case. It defines a relation, but it is also a presentation specification. The resulting presentation may not be a relation (by our restricted definition), even though the resulting rows always form a proper set.

```
FROM my-table
SELECT column-1, column-1, column-1
```

This command defines a *proper* relation consisting of the column named *column-1*, but the presentation layer repeats it three times. Thus the resulting presentation is not a (restricted) relation because there are three columns with the same label.

This `SELECT` does result in a (restricted) relation,

```
FROM my-table
SELECT column-1, column-1 AS Col-2, column-1 AS Col-3
```

---

domains are not necessarily unique. One must bear in mind Codd's work is theoretic. He even points out that he is not designing a data query language. He is providing the foundation upon which to design query languages.

This quibble is for the sake of emphasizing (our) formal definition of *relation*, and to point out when defining a view the `SELECT` command must provide for unique column names. Informally one may consider the results of `SELECT` as a *pseudo-relation.*

Trivially `SELECT` without a `FROM` clause is a one-row relation because Obelisk always assigns unique labels to literals if not otherwise aliased.

```
SELECT 0, ~nomryg-nilref, ~2025.9.24

%obelisk-result:
  %results
    [ %message 'SELECT' ]
    %result-set
      literal-0  literal-1  literal-2
      0  ~nomryg-nilref  ~2025.9.24
    [ %server-time ~2025.9.24..17.56.02..de98 ]
    [ %schema-time ~2025.9.22..22.03.28..6f07 ]
    [ %data-time ~2025.9.22..22.03.28..6f07 ]
    [ %vector-count 1 ]
```

(When there is no `FROM` clause schema and data times reference the creation time of the system database.)

3.3 Joins

The urQL join[16] is restricted to the key words `JOIN`, `CROSS JOIN`, `LEFT JOIN`, `RIGHT JOIN`, `OUTER JOIN`. `JOIN` is either a natural join or a θ-join.[17]

The absence of `ON <predicate>` syntactically determines a natural join, which must adhere to the following rules.

[16] We respect the purity of Codd's original relational algebra, thus there is no *inner join* only join. Outer joins are a set union on a joined relation as well as the remaining rows not being joined (Codd, 1990, p. 107). Nonetheless outer joins have great practical benefit and we opt to dispense with superfluous keywords. Codd never published original research on outer joins, but after their introduction by other authors (Chamberlin and Boyce, 1974), he covered them in a book (Codd, 1990). Oracle is widely credited with the first adoption of outer joins in the early 1980s, and they were first included in the ANSI SQL-92 standard. Outer joins are not included in the first Obelisk beta.

[17] Codd (1970).

Natural join is always between two relations, the subject of the current `JOIN` clause and any relation previously specified in the `FROM` clause, so order of relations matters. The joining characteristic is equality between all like-named and like-typed columns common between the two.[18] Hence a natural join may result in a relation of more rows than either of the two input relations. If there are matching columns with more than one previously listed relation, the join fails and a θ-join is required.

The availability of natural joins encourages transparent and composable schema designs, but bear in mind common metadata columns such as *timestamp* must have uniquely qualified names across tables and views in order for natural joins to be useful.

Syntactically speaking, a θ-join is a join with `ON` `<predicate>` clause wherein at least one equality or inequality operator exists with a column from the current relation on one side and a column from a previously defined relation on the other, and such an operation must exist on both sides of all `OR` conjunctions.

The outer joins `LEFT`, `RIGHT`, and `OUTER` (full outer join) are substantially the same as for any other SQL implementation and may be natural or θ-joins. `CROSS JOIN` is the cartesian join.

3.4 No Nulls

To avoid the quagmire of three-valued (or even four-valued) logic, nulls are entirely banned from urQL.[19] To begin with, columns may not be defined as nullable. This leaves outer joins as the other way traditional SQL database engines can produce nulls. Once again `SELECT` is a special case and does not always produce *ad hoc* relations[20] in SQL or urQL.

[18] Codd (1970) describes this as a cross join filtered for equality on the operands.

[19] Darwen and Date (1998; 2002) influenced this decision.

[20] It is beyond the scope of this paper to invent a new formal definition of *relation*. We imagine that instead of a relation consisting of one tuple type of ordered atomic values, there would be a root tuple type of ordered unique label, type, value triples. (Type ensures strong typing. An untyped version is more general.) Any number of unique sub-types consisting of any subset of

The purpose of a data management system is the organization and retrieval of data. The presentation of that data is an ancillary concern. As a reinvention *from first principles* of relational data management, Obelisk is not obligated to return query results shoehorned into a two-dimensional matrix.

Rather than queries returning column rows of fixed length, Obelisk returns vectors of unique label, type, and atomic datum. The labels—usually the column name from the underlying relation qualified by relation to distinguish like-named columns—and order of the triples are derived from the `SELECT` command. This extends to set operations, notably `UNION`.

Outer joins produce a list of variable length vectors. Let us call each potential variable length a *vector type*. All column name/type labeled values potentially exist in one vector type, and smaller types have a proper subset of these labels in the same order. The upper bound for types in a `LEFT JOIN` or `RIGHT JOIN` is two and for `OUTER JOIN` is three. In the case of set unions the relation types may share no column types whatsoever—in which case there is a hypothetical root type never instantiated.

Presentation software is free to interpret a list of vectors in any manner. By vertically aligning labels, presentation layers are free to insert `NULL` or any other token in holes.

Returning to a previous query example

```
FROM my-table T1
OUTER JOIN my-table AS OF <some past date> T2
WHERE NOT EXISTS T1.key
   OR NOT EXISTS T2.key
SELECT * ;
```

returns the following vector list in pseudo-Hoon:

```
[%vector [p=%t1-key q=[p=~.ud q=1]] [p=%t1-col-2 ...]
 ↳ ...<remaining columns>...]
[%vector [p=%t2-key q=[p=~.ud q=2]] [p=%t2-col-2 ...]
 ↳ ...<remaining columns>...]
```

---

these triples in the same order may also be present. Arranged vertically all the tuples align on label/type matches. Any resulting 2D matrix having more than the root tuple type present has some number of *holes* in every occurrence of a sub-type, and is thus a *sparse relation*.

and in the following section we explain the remaining non-standard attribute of this query.

3.5 Predicate Calculus

To deal with column type sparseness resulting from outer joins and relation unions, urQL introduces two predicate keywords:

- `EXISTS` This is *not* the standard SQL `EXISTS` keyword. Rather it is a unary operator that tests for existence of a column in a possibly sparse relation row, or it can test that a CTE returns data.
- `EQUIV` This binary operator is the same as equality, except comparison of two non-existent columns and/or CTEs results in `TRUE`.

The standard equality and inequality operators comparing any non-existing column and/or CTE results in *false*.

3.6 Relational Integrity

Relational integrity by means of foreign key indices is planned for a future release, substantially following the SQL Standard.

4 Composability

> The universality of the data sublanguage lies in its descriptive ability (Codd, 1970).

```
WITH <ctes>
FROM
<joins>
SCALARS
WHERE
GROUP BY
HAVING
SELECT
ORDER BY
TOP
```

The first rule of Composability Club is, "Have a query syntax that looks compositional." This ordering is the logical flow of data and operations defined by the SQL standard (with a notable Obelisk addition discussed below). It is how users and the database engine agree on constructing proper results. Actual query execution plans may deviate in some way from rigidly following this logical path for performance reasons. This is why, unlike standard SQL, urQL syntax sets the `SELECT` clause in its logical place, not before the `FROM` clause.

4.1 Common Table Expressions

Common Table Expressions (CTEs) entered the SQL standard[21] to make it easier for users to reason about sub-queries. Inlining subqueries makes for bad readability. The SQL Standard must maintain inlining backwards compatibility. urQL has no such constraint. It enforces CTE composability by banning all subquery inlining.

urQL requires a CTE in all cases involving subqueries through runtime validation. Any usage in a predicate or scalar function that can accept a column value or literal also accepts a CTE alias provided that the CTE returns a singleton, one row by one column. This is not the case in the `SELECT` clause. Selecting a singleton CTE is functionally equivalent to a `CROSS JOIN`, which urQL syntax prefers in the interest of explicit programming. Scalar function and predicate operators consuming a list (set) of values require the CTE to return a single column of data.

```
WITH Foo AS (...)
...
WHERE bar IN Foo
```

4.2 Scalar Functions

Scalar functions present another opportunity to enforce composability. The `SCALARS` keyword introduces a clause where all scalar functions must be defined. They are subsequently referenced by alias. A scalar function operates on any data in

[21]The ANSI/ISO SQL standard defined Common Table Expressions in 1999.

a single data row as well as singleton and list CTEs and returns one consistently typed value.

```
SCALARS
  Sc1 IF foo = 1 THEN bar ELSE foobar END-IF
  Sc2 IF Sc1 = 'what-not' THEN %.y ELSE %.n END-IF
  Sc3 IF Sc2 THEN dt-col ELSE ~2025.9.6 END-IF
```

In legacy SQL this would all be nested and inlined in a `SELECT` clause or predicate. In urQL one inlines the scalar alias.

Obelisk supports `IF`, `CASE`, `COALESCE`, and many other common SQL scalar functions.

5 Security

The Urbit architecture provides for single sign-on (SSO) through the immutable identity of all computers on the network. Obelisk security[22] allows for grouping identities, much like security on other SQL database implementations. In addition parent, child, and sibling are predefined groups providing for subnet security. The Urbit network architecture provides for subnets with two levels of hierarchy—parent, a ship of identity type *galaxy*, *star*, or *planet*, and children, ships of identity type *moon*.

User permissions are for *ships* (computers) on the network, for *agents* (userspace programs), or a combination of the two.[23] Permissions can be any combination of whitelists or blacklists affecting databases, namespaces, tables and views, or columns. Permissions may be read-only or for write affecting data. Schema read is allowed, but update can only be performed by the host ship. Whitelisting and blacklisting can be tailored by timeframe, both in regards to the data or schema state permitted or restricted and the effective time range of the permission itself.

Obelisk, like other SQL-based relational databases, is susceptible to SQL injection attacks, and the mitigation for Obelisk

[22]Not in the first beta release. The first beta prevents all access by a foreign ship.

[23]Userspace security is still a work in progress in the Urbit architecture.

is the same as for other DBMSs—implementing stored procedures and adding a level of SP permissions.

Short of dropping a database, any write—even dropping a table—results in a new state. Referencing a prior state and writing to it (with proper planning) can effectively correct any destructive write.

Obelisk security is believed to be robust up to disk and RAM hacking.

6 The Shrubbery

Key to Codd's invention of the relational database is his critique of hierarchical databases.[24] It took another 20 years to mostly fulfill the demise of accessing data via paths. Yet the concept lingers and is not without merit. Urbit being both a computer fundamentally supporting a hierarchical (tree) architecture and a network of nodes with immutable identities is the perfect substrate for implementing a truly global namespace.[25]

Obelisk fully supports global namespace access to data and schema. This urQL/Obelisk functionality is not easily duplicated on computers other than Urbit.

```
SELECT DATABASE animal-shelter
```

`SELECT DATABASE` returns the entire *animal-shelter*[26] noun.[27]

[24]Codd (1970), "1.1.3 Access Path Dependence". Codd uses the term *data store* which is mostly interchangeable with *database*, even if they conjure up different images in the mind.

[25]Not in the first beta release. The shrubbery concept of a universal namespace is an organic outgrowth of the Urbit file system (Clay). Within Urbit circles the concept is still amorphous. It could be more than an Urbit network URI, with endpoints functioning as data or software. It is hard to identify a single author or inventor. `~rovnys-ricfer` originated the term in conversation with `~littel-wolfur` and was the first to write about it (`~rovnys-ricfer`, personal communication, ~2025.10.18; `~rovnys-ricfer`, undated). `~sarpen-laplux` developed the earliest working implementation in 2023. `~hastuc-dibtux` subsequently carried out extensive prototyping and advocacy (2024). `~migrev-dolseg`'s `%hawk` Gall app is the most readily available and extensive implementation in this tradition to date (2025).

[26]Levin (2020) Available for several database platforms, this is a readily available non-trivial sample database that demonstrates natural primary table keys.

[27]Backups may be implemented as a copy of the database noun on an-

Formatted as a path in the global Urbit namespace (beginning with ship identity)

```
/~nomryg-nilref/obelisk/animal-shelter
```

any caller on the network with sufficient security permissions can retrieve a copy of the database.

Working our way down the schema hierarchy we have access to namespaces within a database,

```
SELECT NAMESPACE animal-shelter.reference
```

```
~/obelisk/animal-shelter/reference
```

and pause to point out the path is on the local ship, but still confined by local desk[28] permissions. The returned noun is all the user defined tables, views, and indices in the selected namespace, including all their schema and data states.

```
SELECT my-table
```

```
~/obelisk/db1/dbo/my-table
```

The reader may wonder about the syntax here. Submission of urQL scripts to the Obelisk parser requires the name of a default database along with the script, and `dbo` is always the default namespace. The returned noun is the same metadata and result set whose print format we have seen above.

We cannot tell from the syntax (or the returned metadata) whether the query returned the data from a table or view. Views can shadow tables. To force a table add the `TABLE` keyword to the script, or in the namespace,

```
~/obelisk/db1/dbo/table/my-table
```

and use `AS OF` for a particular state,

```
~/obelisk/db1/dbo/my-table/~2020.1.26
```

The final drill down in the namespace is to the column level,

---

other ship. The Urbit computer is already an ACID database and nouns are de-duplicated on the same ship. So references to the same noun are pointers to the single physical occurrence of that noun.

[28] A *desk* can be thought of as an application space inside of userspace.

```
SELECT db1..my-table.column-4
~/obelisk/db1/dbo/my-table/column-4
```

Keep in mind Obelisk returns proper sets of data rows. Only a view is capable of deterministic ordering of the result rows when accessing data in this manner.

Shrubbery support provides for hybrid relational/hierarchical data processing. The Hawk Urbit implementation of namespace computing provides for scripting language or API usage of Obelisk as well as path access and post processing. There is already a working adaptation of a SQL Studio-like interface to Obelisk available in Hawk.

7 Data Structures

> Bad programmers worry about the code. Good programmers worry about data structures and their relationships (Torvalds, 2016).

To better understand the workings of Obelisk we turn to the data structures. Obelisk is a work in progress approaching a beta release, so some structures still may change over time.

7.1 AST/API

The Obelisk parser parses urQL commands into the structures in file `/sur/ast`, which also serves as the Obelisk API. We show the most important schema and content manipulating commands in Figure 1. A `qualified-column` is one qualified by a `qualified-table`.

```
:: create-database
$:  %create-database
    name=@tas
    as-of=(unit as-of)
==

:: drop-database
$:  %drop-database
    name=@tas
    force=?
==

:: create-namespace
$:  %create-namespace
    database-name=@tas
    name=@tas
    as-of=(unit as-of)
==

:: create-table
$:  %create-table
    table=qualified-table
    columns=(list column)
    pri-indx=(list ordered-column)
    foreign-keys=(list foreign-key)
    as-of=(unit as-of)
==

:: predicate
(tree predicate-component)
```

```
:: qualified-table
$:  %qualified-table
    ship=(unit @p)
    database=@tas
    namespace=@tas
    name=@tas
    alias=(unit @t)
==

:: drop-table
$:  %drop-table
    table=qualified-table
    force=?
    as-of=(unit as-of)
==

:: update
$:  %update
    ctes=(list cte)
    table=qualified-table
    as-of=(unit as-of)
    $:  columns=(list qualified-column)
        values=(list value-or-default)
    ==
    =predicate
==
```

```
:: delete
$:  %delete
    ctes=(list cte)
    table=qualified-table
    as-of=(unit as-of)
    =predicate
==

:: truncate-table
$:  %truncate-table
    table=qualified-table
    as-of=(unit as-of)
==

:: predicate-component
 $? ops-and-conjs
   qualified-column
   unqualified-column
   dime
   value-literals
    cte-alias
    scalar-alias
    aggregate
==

:: column
$:  %column
    name=@tas
    type=@ta
==
```

Figure 1: Obelisk schema creation and modification AST/API structures, from /sur/ast.

Obelisk does not yet support interacting with tables on foreign ships, so qualification is currently only by database and namespace. An alias may be assigned in the urQL. There is no distinction in urQL or the AST between tables and views. A view may shadow a table in the context of queries, but schema and data manipulating commands always operate on the specified table.

We see that `DELETE` requires a predicate (unlike standard SQL) and the predicate data structure is tree-shaped. Predicate nodes are operators, conjunctions, or any number of representations of data.

Figure 2 presents the `selection` data structure, also a tree structure which accommodates either a set operator or one of three other structures as nodes. `insert` and `merge` are for future implementation using the `%into` operator. The `query` data structure is central to reading and formatting persisted data and can be combined with any of the regular set operators (`%union`, `%except`, `%intersect`, `%divided-by`). If there are CTEs, they are processed first to return one relation each. Prior CTE relations are accessible by subsequent CTEs. Internally different kinds of relation data structure represent data returned by CTEs (`cte-alias`) or more commonly `qualified-table`, which includes (possibly table-shadowing) views. (`query-row` is a placeholder for future temporary table urQL syntax.)

```
:: selection
$:  %selection
    ctes=(list cte)
    set-functions=(tree set-function)
==

:: set-function
$?(set-cmd set-op)

:: query
$:  %query
    from=(unit from)
    scalars=(list scalar)
    =predicate
    group-by=(list grouping-column)
    having=predicate
    =select
    order-by=(list ordering-column)
==

:: set-op
$?  %union
    %except
    %intersect
    %divided-by
    %divide-with-remainder
    %into
==

:: set-cmd
$%(insert merge query)

:: cte
$:  %cte
    name=@tas
    =query
==

:: from
$:  %from
    =relation
    as-of=(unit as-of)
    joins=(list joined-object)
==

:: scalar
$:  %scalar
    scalar=scalar-function
    alias=@t
==

:: select
$:  %select
    top=(unit @ud)
    columns=(list selected-column)
==

:: selected-column
$%  qualified-column
    unqualified-column
    selected-aggregate
    selected-value
    selected-all
    selected-all-object
==

:: insert
$:  %insert
    table=qualified-table
    as-of=(unit as-of)
    columns=(unit (list @tas))
    values=insert-values
==

:: relation
$%  qualified-table
    cte-alias
    query-row
==

:: joined-object
$:  %joined-object
    join=join-type
    =relation
    as-of=(unit as-of)
    =predicate
==
```

Figure 2: Obelisk query and selection AST/API structures, from /sur/ast.

`selected-column` deals with all the different ways columns and data may be selected in urQL, qualified and unqualified columns, literals, all columns across all joins, and all columns of a specified relation. (Aggregate functions are for a future release.)

A potential enhancement to the urQL syntax and AST in a future release is to support zero-ary structures in the `SELECT` clause of a query. This is an area of research enabled by Obelisk's ability to produce result vectors and sub-vectors (see outer joins above). The model is how the Datalog language defines zero-ary structures, beginning a sub-structure with `:-` colhep and ending it with a `.` dot, allowing nested substructures.

The example

```
SELECT column-1, column-2, :- column-3, column-4.,
 ↳ column-5
```

would return one `vector` of `column-1`, `column-2`, `column-5`, and one `vector` of `column-3`, `column-4` for every instance of the same `column-1`, `column-2`, `column-5`. This would open the door to returning complex nouns from queries.

7.2 Persistence Layer

At the very top of the Persistence Layer (Figure3) is the server data structure.

```
+$  server  (map @tas database)
```

This is simply an index into all the databases, including the `%sys` database tracking other databases. This is the noun which the Obelisk app persists. Alternate implementations using an app structure other than the one provided with Obelisk merely need to persist this noun.

```
:: database
$:  %database
    name=@tas
    created-provenance=path
    created-tmsp=@da
    sys=((mop @da schema) gth)
    content=((mop @da dataa) gth)
    =view-cache
==

:: view-cache
((mop ns-obj-key cache) ns-obj-comp)

:: ns-obj-key
$:  ns=@tas
    obj=@tas
    time=@da
==

:: cache
$:  %cache
    tmsp=@da
    content=(unit cache-content)
==

:: ns-obj-comp
|=  [p=data-obj-key q=data-obj-key]
^-  ?

:: cache-content
$:  rowcount=@
    rows=(list (map @tas @))
==

:: schema
$:  %schema
    provenance=path
    tmsp=@da
    =namespaces
    tables=(map [@tas @tas] table)
    views=((mop data-obj-key view)
      ns-obj-comp)
==

:: data
$:  %data
    ship=@p
    provenance=path
    tmsp=@da
    files=(map [@tas @tas] file)
==

:: table
$:  %table
    provenance=path
    tmsp=@da
    =column-lookup
    type-lookup=(map @tas @ta)
    pri-indx=index
    columns=(list column)
    indices=(list index)
==

:: column-lookup
(map @tas [aura @])

:: view
$:  %view
    provenance=path
    tmsp=@da
    =selection
    =column-lookup
    type-lookup=(map @tas @ta)
    columns=(list column)
    ordering=(list column-order)
==
```

Figure 3: Obelisk persistence layer AST/API structures, from /sur/server-state. (Continues on next page.)

```
:: file
$:  %file
    ship=@p
    provenance=path
    tmsp=@da
    =column-addrs
    rowcount=@
    pri-idx=(tree [(list @) (map @tas @)])
    indexed-rows=(list indexed-row)
    =column-catalog
==
```

```
:: indexed-row
$:  %indexed-row
    key=(list @)
    data=(map @tas @)
==
::
```

Figure 3: Obelisk persistence layer AST/API structures, from /sur/server-state. (Continued from previous page.)

The `database` structure reveals the simplicity of Obelisk time-travel. The database schema and content are both +mops (ordered +maps) indexed by time. The magic of Urbit noun de-duplication does the rest.

`view-cache` provides for fast retrieval of view data after a view has been requested once. Any alteration of table data underlying a view will create a new entry keyed on namespace, view name, and time, but without content. The first request for that key will cause the entire `selection` to execute and save the content. There are currently only system views. User-defined views will be in a later release.

`table` defines the schema used to persist data for a persisted relation. `'column-lookup'` returns the column type (aura) as well as its position in the canonical ordering. `tables` require a unique primary index, and for now there are no secondary table indices.

```
+$  index
    $:  %index
        unique=?
        key=(list key-column)
==  ==
+$  key-column
    $:  %key-column
      name=@tas
      =aura
      ascending=?
==  ==
```

```
::  action
$%  $:  %tape
        default-database=@tas
        urql=tape
    ==
    $:  %commands
        cmds=(list command)
==  ==

::  cmd-result
$:  %results
    (list result)
==

::  vector
$:  %vector
    (lest vector-cell)
==

::  vector-cell
[p=@tas q=dime]
```

```
::  result
$%  [%message msg=@t]
    [%vector-count count=@ud]
    [%server-time date=@da]
    [%security-time date=@da]
    [%schema-time date=@da]
    [%data-time date=@da]
    [%result-set (list vector)]
==
```

```
::  command
$%  alter-index
    alter-namespace
    alter-table
    create-database
    create-index
    create-namespace
    create-table
    create-view
    delete
    drop-database
    drop-index
    drop-namespace
    drop-table
    drop-view
    grant
    revoke
    selection
    truncate-table
    update
==
```

Figure 4: Obelisk presentation layer AST/API structures, from `/sur/obelisk`.

`columns` returns the columns in canonical order (the order originally defined).

With the table definition established, the actual data is in a `file` structure, also containing relevant metadata. At the most basic level, every row of persisted data consists of a key—a list of atoms which is one or more of the subsequent columns, and the column data, which maps from column name to the atomic value. Of all the persistence layer structures, the one actually persisting data is probably the most prone to future development. For purposes of alternating query execution plans, data is persisted in more than one way. `(tree [(list @) (map @tas @)])` is an ordered map allowing ordered selection on partial keys. `column-catalog` is a currently abandoned attempt at persisting data column-wise. (Inserting large amounts of data stored column-wise proved impractical, so for now column-wise storage is deferred.) `indexed-rows` is the only form currently in use, so for the beta release every query plan execution is a table scan.

7.3 Presentation Layer

Aside from urQL, Obelisk users only ever interact with the presentation layer (Figure 4). The Obelisk app allows for two actions, `%tape`, which submits a command and default database name in a urQL `$tape`, and `%commands`, which is a list of API commands where every table and view is already fully qualified by database.

This section has covered most of the available commands; several planned commands like alters, drops, and security commands will parse but are not yet supported in the Obelisk engine.

Every urQL command returns a result structure of metadata and vectors, which we have already covered.

An untapped area of investigation is to change the `%result-set` from returning `(list vector)` to returning a `list` of trap cores which emit `vector` when evaluated. The lookup of columns row by row in the query relation is computationally intense and could be offloaded to the client side.

8 Conclusion

A database scripting language should provide the most intuitive and complete experience possible for organizing and querying data. Uniting the relational data model with set theory and predicate calculus has proven to be the most effective general means of organizing and retrieving data to date, however the hierarchical model still has its place and should be supported as far as possible. We have seen that even SQL databases have at least a three-level hierarchy, four including namespaces, five when implemented as a temporal database.

Obelisk and its urQL scripting language represent a reimagining of the relational database paradigm, inspired by and tailored to the unique architecture of the Urbit computer while remaining adaptable to other computing environments and free of the constraints of SQL's backward compatibility, Obelisk leverages E. F. Codd's foundational principles to address longstanding deficiencies in traditional RDBMSs. Its innovations—time travel through database states, idempotent queries, proper set operations, elimination of nulls, and enforced composability—offer a streamlined, transparent, and powerful approach to data management. The integration of Urbit's pure functional model ensures that all operations, whether through the urQL scripting language or the API, are consistent and accessible, with no hidden functionality. Additionally, through Urbit's global hierarchical namespace, data access via namespace path enhances flexibility, while Urbit's identity-based security model provides robust protection. Obelisk not only advances the state of relational databases but also sets a new standard for clarity, consistency, and innovation in structured data systems.

Appendix: Examples

```
/* The %sys database contains provenance metadata for
all the user databases.
*/

FROM sys.sys.databases
SELECT database, sys-agent, sys-tmsp, data-ship,
       data-agent, data-tmsp ;

/* Set the default database to animal-shelter for the
remaining queries. The rest of the schema metadata is
in %sys namespace views of each user database.
*/

FROM sys.tables
SELECT namespace, name, agent, tmsp, row-count ;

FROM sys.columns
SELECT namespace, name, col-ordinal, col-name,
 ↳ col-type ;

/* The %sys namespace views also tracks the schema and
content history.
*/

FROM sys.sys-log SELECT tmsp, agent, component, name ;

FROM sys.data-log
SELECT tmsp, ship, agent, namespace, table, row-count ;

/* Start exploring. Return complete sentences,
  if you like.
*/

FROM reference.calendar T1
JOIN reference.calendar-us-fed-holiday T2
WHERE T1.date BETWEEN ~2025.1.1
      AND ~2025.12.31
SELECT 'On this day: ', day-name, ',', T1.date,
 ↳     ', is the holiday ', us-federal-holiday, '.' ;
```

```
/* Create a new database, add a table and insert data.
The default namespace is %dbo.
*/

CREATE DATABASE db2 AS OF ~2000.1.1 ;

CREATE TABLE db2..my-table-1 (col1 @t, col2 @da)
PRIMARY KEY (col1) ;

INSERT INTO db2..my-table-1 (col1, col2)
  VALUES ('today', ~2000.1.1)
    ('tomorrow', ~2000.1.2)
    ('next-day', ~2000.1.3)
    ('next-today', ~2000.1.1)
    ('next-tomorrow', ~2000.1.2)
    ('next-next-day', ~2000.1.3) ;
```

References

Chamberlin, Donald D. and Raymond F. Boyce (1974). "SEQUEL: A Structured English Query Language." In: *SIGFIDET '74: Proceedings of the 1974 ACM SIGFIDET (now SIGMOD) Workshop on Data Description, Access and Control*, pp. 249–264. URL: https://doi.org/10.1145/800296.811515 (visited on ~2025.9.5).

Codd, E. F. (1970). *A Relational Model of Data for Large Shared Data Banks*. Tech. rep. San Jose, California: IBM Research Laboratory. URL: https://www.seas.upenn.edu/~zives/03f/cis550/codd.pdf (visited on ~2025.9.5).

— (1990). *The Relational Model for Database Management: Version 2*. Addison-Wesley.

Darwen, Hugh and C. J. Date (1998). *Databases, Types, and the Relational Model: The Third Manifesto*. Revised 2006. Addison-Wesley.

— (2002). *Temporal Data and the Relational Model*. Morgan Kaufmann.

~hastuc-dibtux, Liam Fitzgerald (2024) "Shrub". URL: https://github.com/urbit/shrub (visited on ~2025.9.27).

Levin, Ami (2020) "Animal Shelter". URL: https://github.com/ami-levin/Animal_Shelter (visited on ~2025.9.13).

~migrev-dolseg, William Hanlen (2025) "ways hawk is practically useful for me, right now". URL: https://willhanlen.com/~~/outbox/25/7/my-hawk-uses/ (visited on ~2025.9.8).

~rovnys-ricfer, Theodore Blackman (n. d., ca. 2023) "Young Shrub". URL: https://rovnys.cataphract.us/young-shrub (visited on ~2025.9.8).

~sorreg-namtyv, Curtis Yarvin et al. (2016). *Urbit: A Solid-State Interpreter.* Whitepaper. Tlon Corporation. URL: https://media.urbit.org/whitepaper.pdf (visited on ~2024.1.25).

A noun is an atom or a cell. An atom is a natural number.
A cell is an ordered pair of nouns.

Reduce by the first matching pattern; variables match any noun.

```
nock(a)             *a
[a b c]             [a [b c]]

?[a b]              0
?a                  1
+[a b]              +[a b]
+a                  1 + a
=[a a]              0
=[a b]              1

/[1 a]              a
/[2 a b]            a
/[3 a b]            b
/[(a + a) b]        /[2 /[a b]]
/[(a + a + 1) b]    /[3 /[a b]]
/a                  /a

#[1 a b]            a
#[(a + a) b c]      #[a [b /[(a + a + 1) c]] c]
#[(a + a + 1) b c]  #[a [/[(a + a) c] b] c]
#a                  #a

*[a [b c] d]        [*[a b c] *[a d]]

*[a 0 b]            /[b a]
*[a 1 b]            b
*[a 2 b c]          *[*[a b] *[a c]]
*[a 3 b]            ?*[a b]
*[a 4 b]            +*[a b]
*[a 5 b c]          =[*[a b] *[a c]]

*[a 6 b c d]        *[a *[[c d] 0 *[[2 3] 0 *[a 4 4 b]]]]
*[a 7 b c]          *[*[a b] c]
*[a 8 b c]          *[[*[a b] a] c]
*[a 9 b c]          *[*[a c] 2 [0 1] 0 b]
*[a 10 [b c] d]     #[b *[a c] *[a d]]

*[a 11 [b c] d]     *[[*[a c] *[a d]] 0 3]
*[a 11 b c]         *[a c]

*a                  *a
```

www.ingramcontent.com/pod-product-compliance
Lightning Source LLC
LaVergne TN
LVHW040515210926
848480LV00005BA/1471
9798295448638